A

G

S
1

Ji

Hodder & Stoughton

A MEMBER OF THE HODDER HEADLINE GROUP

The cover illustration shows Philip IV of Spain by Velasquez (Courtesy M.A.S. Barcelona)

Some other titles in the series:

Luther and the German Reformation, 1517–55
Keith Randell   ISBN 0 340 51808 1
John Calvin and the Later Reformation
Keith Randell   ISBN 0 340 52940 7
The Catholic and Counter Reformations
Keith Randell   ISBN 0 340 53495 8
From Revolt to Independence: The Netherlands 1550–1650
Martyn Rady   ISBN 0 340 51803 0
The Unification of Italy, 1815–70
Andrina Stiles   ISBN 0 340 51809 X
The Unification of Germany, 1815–90
Andrina Stiles   ISBN 0 340 51810 3

Order: Please contact Bookpoint Ltd, 130 Milton Park, Abingdon, Oxon OX14 4SB. Telephone: (44) 01235 827720. Fax: (44) 01235 400454. Lines are open from 9 am – 6 pm Monday to Saturday, with a 24-hour message answering service. You can also order through our website at www.hodderheadline.co.uk

British Library Cataloguing in Publication Data

Kilsby, Jill
    Spain: Rise and Decline, 1474-1463.
    (Access to History).
    1. Spain-History-Ferdinand and Isabella, 1479-1515   2. Spain-History-house of Austria, 1516-1700
    I. Title   II. Series
    940′.04   DP161

ISBN 0–340–51807-3

First published in Access to A-Level History series 1986. Three impressions
This edition published 1989
Impression number   18   17   16   15   14   13   12
Year   2004   2003

Printed in Great Britain for Hodder & Stoughton Educational, a division of Hodder Headline, 338 Euston Road, London NW1 3BH by The Bath Press, Bath

Contents

Preface

To the general reader

Although the *Access to History* series has been designed with the needs of students studying the subject at higher examination levels very much in mind, it also has a great deal to offer the general reader. The main body of the text (i.e. ignoring the Study Guides at the ends of chapters) forms a readable and yet stimulating survey of a coherent topic as studied by historians. However, each author's aim has not merely been to provide a clear explanation of what happened in the past (to interest and inform); it has also been assumed that most readers wish to be stimulated into thinking further about the topic and to form opinions of their own about the significance of the events that are described and discussed (to be challenged). Thus, although no prior knowledge of the topic is expected on the reader's part, she or he is treated as an intelligent and thinking person throughout. The author tends to share ideas and possibilities with the reader, rather than passing on numbers of so-called 'historical truths'.

To the student reader

There are many ways in which the series can be used by students studying History at a higher level. It will, therefore, be worthwhile thinking about your own study strategy before you start your work on this book. Obviously, your strategy will vary depending on the aim you have in mind, and the time for study that is available to you.

If, for example, you want to acquire a general overview of the topic in the shortest possible time, the following approach will probably be the most effective:

1. Read Chapter 1 and think about its contents.
2. Read the 'Making notes' section at the end of Chapter 2 and decide whether it is necessary for you to read this chapter.
3. If it is, read the chapter, stopping at each heading or ★ to note down the main points that have been made.
4. Repeat stage 2 (and stage 3 where appropriate) for all the other chapters.

If, however, your aim is to gain a thorough grasp of the topic, taking however much time is necessary to do so, you may benefit from carrying out the same procedure with each chapter, as follows:

1. Read the chapter as fast as you can, and preferably at one sitting.
2. Study the flow diagram at the end of the chapter, ensuring that you understand the general 'shape' of what you have just read.
3. Read the 'Making notes' section (and the 'Answering essay

questions' section, if there is one) and decide what further work you need to do on the chapter. In particularly important sections of the book, this will involve reading the chapter a second time and stopping at each heading and * to think about (and to write a summary of) what you have just read.

4. Attempt the 'Source-based questions' section. It will sometimes be sufficient to think through your answers, but additional understanding will often be gained by forcing yourself to write them down.

When you have finished the main chapters of the book, study the 'Further Reading' section and decide what additional reading (if any) you will do on the topic.

This book has been designed to help make your studies both enjoyable and successful. If you can think of ways in which this could have been done more effectively, please write to tell me. In the meantime, I hope that you will gain greatly from your study of History.

Keith Randell

A Note on Money

In Castile accounting was done in *maravedis* up to the sixteenth century. Accounts were then kept in ducats. One ducat was worth 375 *maravedis*.

CHAPTER 1

Introduction, Spain: Rise and Decline, 1474–1643

1 The Geographical Background

When British people of today think of Spain they tend to have in mind that part of the coast that borders the Mediterranean and which many seek every August for its 'sun, sand and sea'. This, however, is only one part of Spain. Another coast borders the Atlantic Ocean. One land frontier is marked by the Pyrenees, and the other by modern day Portugal. Together Spain and Portugal make up the Iberian Peninsula. Though a part of Europe, it is very much a distinct unit. There are no easy channels of communications with the other countries of Europe. On the other hand only 19 kilometres separate it from the coast of North Africa. The peninsula is therefore at a crossroads, between the Mediterranean Sea and the Atlantic one way, and the mainland of Europe and Africa the other.

This is not to say that within that peninsula the areas that form modern day Spain and Portugal enjoy close links. Geographical factors prevent this being so. A look at any map showing the geographical features of the country illustrates the main reasons for this very clearly. Around the edge is a narrow coastal plain. But a short journey into the interior quickly reveals rivers, valleys and, in particular, mountains. Spain is Europe's most mountainous country after Switzerland. Over one sixth of the country is more than 1000 metres above sea level. The most important geographical feature in the interior is the Meseta, the enormous plateau at its centre. This is almost completely surrounded by high mountain ranges and is therefore remote from both the sea and the neighbouring countries of Portugal and France.

Extremes of climate are to be met. In the Meseta long, hard winters are followed by short periods of intense heat – what some Spaniards of today refer to as 'nine months of winter and three of hell'. The areas near the Pyrenees are, in contrast, much wetter with no extremes of temperature. The east and south coast are different again. Here it is very hot with little in the way of a winter, but the area suffers from a lack of rain.

Such conditions make a country in which food cannot easily be grown. In almost every part of Spain, apart from the river valleys and the narrow coastal plains, there are many areas where crop yields are too poor to provide enough food to sustain a large population. It is not surprising therefore, as the Spanish historian Pierre Vilar has shown, that so many of the maritime areas of Spain have sought to build up trade overseas – across the Mediterranean, over to Africa, or towards the Atlantic – rather than with the less productive central area.

The geography of the peninsula partly explains the way in which the political units in the area came to be formed as they did. Three main divisions can be distinguished: the area forming Portugal, that making Castile, and those regions which comprised the Crown of Aragon. However, there was no Kingdom of Spain as there was a Kingdom of Portugal. The word 'Spain' was not widely used by those living in the peninsula in the mid-fifteenth century, although there may have been some who referred to themselves as Spanish. Certainly many foreigners called the people who lived in the Iberian Peninsula by this name. But most of the population thought of themselves as coming from particular parts of the peninsula, as being from Castile, Aragon, Catalonia, Navarre or Portugal. They called themselves not Spanish but Castilians, Aragonese, Catalans, or Portuguese. It was not, however, just geographical factors which led to these groupings. The political history of the various regions also contributed.

2 The Historical Background

The only time the Iberian Peninsula had been a single political unit was when it was a province of the Roman Empire – Roman Hispania. It was during this period that it became Christianised. However, in the eighth century, Muslims from North Africa crossed to the peninsula and conquered it. Two centuries later, the Christians recaptured part of the north of Spain, and from the eleventh century onwards began to move south on a slow but definite Reconquest. By the end of the thirteenth century, only the Kingdom of Granada remained under Muslim rulers.

The Reconquest had partly been a desire to re-establish Christian rule. At the same time, increases in population among Christians in the north, and subsequent pressure on food supplies, had led to a need to expand and acquire more land.

By the end of the thirteenth century, three major Christian kingdoms had formed in the peninsula. Castile and Leon had come under one Christian king; Portugal had become an independent kingdom, and the Pyrenean kingdoms of Catalonia, Aragon and Valencia had amalgamated to become the Crown of Aragon. The small kingdom of Navarre mainly governed itself, although in some matters it was subject to Castile. At the same time, even within these units, there remained great varieties of customs and laws.

The warlike existence of the kingdoms had meant that the nobility, which provided the military leadership in each, held a position of importance. This was true of Castile in particular. The nobles there were frontiersmen who fought and won large areas of land from the Muslims. To help in the struggle, three religious orders of knights had been formed in the twelfth century – Calatrava, Alcantara and Santiago – whose task was to defend the frontier bordering Muslim territory.

* While most of Castile's interests had been involved in the

See Preface for explanation of * symbol.

The Iberian Peninsula in the fifteenth, sixteenth and seventeenth centuries

Reconquest, from the twelfth century, Aragon had begun to direct its energies beyond the peninsula and into the Mediterranean. Majorca and all the Balearic Islands had been conquered. Further conquests had followed over the next two centuries. The most important of these were Sicily, Sardinia and Naples (see map on page 35). Aragon had also taken control of a number of fortified towns in North Africa. Barcelona, in Catalonia, became one of the most important ports in the Western Mediterranean. The first Spanish overseas empire had been founded and Spanish interest in Italy had been established.

* Aragon's power did not last. By the middle of the fifteenth century it was clear that Castile would be the more important in the future. There were several reasons for this. Firstly, Castile was four times larger in size than Aragon. Its population was also greater, possibly five million people in contrast to Aragon's one million. Castile was more unified. It possessed only one *Cortes* (or parliament), one language, one coinage, and one administration. Its economy had begun to thrive. Trade was mainly in raw materials, above all wool. The wool trade was controlled by the *Mesta* which was a group of all the producers of wool in Castile. Exports were sent to the markets of Northern Europe, particularly Flanders in the Netherlands, where Castilian merchants played a leading role. The ports through which such exports went also co-operated. In Aragon, in contrast, there was no such economic unity. Towns even competed against each other for trade as much as against any rivals outside Aragon. Much economic damage was done to Aragon by a lengthy civil war. In addition, the major port in the realm, Barcelona, was hit by an economic crisis which affected most of the Mediterranean ports after 1350, and which led to bankruptcies and unemployment.

3 The Institutions of Aragon and Castile

Just as Aragon and Castile had developed in different ways so there were different institutions within the two realms. The Crown of Aragon consisted mainly of the three separate kingdoms of Catalonia, Aragon and Valencia. Each was governed independently, had its own laws and its own Cortes. In contrast, Castile consisted of a number of former kingdoms which held their institutions in common. There were, however, even in Castile, areas which had a great deal of independence. Although the Basque provinces recognised the sovereignty of the King of Castile, they were otherwise almost independent. The Asturias and Galicia had their own regional governments. In other parts of Castile there were local privileges, particularly those held by the nobility.

  * The Cortes was the means by which the political views of the important people in the country were heard. However, the powers held by the Cortes in each of the kingdoms were very different. In Aragon the various Cortes sometimes met at the same time and in the same city (*Cortes generales*). More frequently they met separately in their own kingdoms. All laws in the Crown of Aragon (meaning all the kingdoms in Aragon) had to be approved by the individual Cortes. The monarch's powers for administering justice, imposing taxes or raising armies were all severely limited by the *fueros* (the laws and privileges possessed by these kingdoms). These were defended by the *justicia* – a law officer with wide powers, who could not be removed from office by the king. In Castile, in contrast, the Cortes was weak, and had few powers to prevent a ruler from doing as he or she wished. The crown here had the right to make and unmake laws without the consent of the Cortes.

4 Religion

By the mid-fifteenth century the main religion in the peninsula was Christianity, although there were large communities of both Muslims and Jews. All three felt that they had to co–exist if they were to survive. At times of peace during the Reconquest, it had been common for Muslims and Christians to visit each other, to trade and even to inter-marry. A writer in thirteenth century Castile was able to say:

1   there is war between the Christians and the Moors, [Muslims from
    North Africa] and there will be, until the Christians have got back
    the lands which the Moors took from them by force, for neither
    because of the law [i.e. faith] nor because of the sect that they hold
5   to, would there be war against them.

Within the Christian territories Jews mainly lived in the towns. Here
they were often leading financiers, lending to both the kings of Aragon
and those of Castile. One king of Aragon claimed that, 'our predecessors
have tolerated and suffered the Jews in their territories because these
Jews are the strong box and treasury of the kings'. Many Jews were
important in trade and in professions such as medicine. The Muslims, on
the other hand, were mainly to be found in the countryside.

* The Christian victories of the Reconquest altered the relationship
between the three religious groupings. Although the rulers might continue to show support for Jews and Muslims, there was a general hostility
towards them, particularly during times of economic depression and
epidemics. Most Jews suffered increasingly during the fourteenth
century from pogroms (organised massacres). Many were forcibly converted to Christianity. They were then known as *conversos* or 'new'
Christians to distinguish them from those who had been Christians for
many generations – the 'old' Christians.

5 The Growth of the Empire

By the middle of the fifteenth century Castile was in a position from
which she could become an important power in Europe. The marriage of
Ferdinand of Aragon and Isabella of Castile in 1469 brought most of the
peninsula under the same rulers. Other marriages were to further extend
the Spanish Empire, or Monarchy, as it was called to distinguish it from
the Holy Roman Empire (a collection of hundreds of states in the lands
which today make up Germany and beyond). In 1496 two portentous
marriages were arranged: those of two children of Ferdinand and Isabella
with two children of the Holy Roman Emperor, Maximilian.

Maximilian was the head of the Habsburg family, whose lands lay
mainly in Austria. In 1438 a member of this family had become Holy
Roman Emperor and from then on members of the family were to hold
the title continuously. However, although the title brought prestige, it
brought little power. Power came from the lands they had acquired
through a series of advantageous marriage alliances. In 1477 Maximilian
had married Mary of Burgundy. As a result he had obtained much
additional land, including Artois, Franche–Comté and the Netherlands. During the early sixteenth century he was also to inherit Bohemia
and western Hungary.

The marriages of two of the Habsburg children to two of those of
Ferdinand and Isabella were eventually to bring a Habsburg to the

thrones of Aragon and Castile in the person of Charles I. Charles I was also to inherit the Habsburg lands in northern and central Europe and thereby not only extended his Empire considerably but also brought Spanish involvement in the affairs of Northern Europe.

Charles's son, Philip II, was to inherit the Habsburg lands in Italy, the Netherlands, Spain and Spain's empire in America, which had been discovered during the reign of Ferdinand and Isabella, and had grown considerably in size by the mid-sixteenth century. In addition he became ruler of Portugal and acquired the vast Portuguese empire in the East. In 1620 a Castilian wrote:

1   Now that to the Crown of Spain there have been added Aragon, Portugal, Navarre, and all that is beautiful and splendid in Italy, Flanders, Lombardy, the East and the West Indies, such that with its land and its sea it lies along the whole path of the sun and the sun
5   is scarcely lost to view from this monarchy, now that it is superior in Territories, in riches, unequalled by those of Antiquity, superior in valour, loyalty, and the troth it keeps with its princes, and in firm religion and unswerving devotion to the church . . . the Ambassador of Spain has a patent claim everywhere and always to lay claim
10   to precedence.

Similar words could equally well have been used forty years earlier.

*   The mere size of the lands over which Charles and his successors ruled was to lead to difficulties. The increased power which it gave them led to the Habsburg name being feared and envied throughout this period by the other powers of Europe, particularly France. All countries in Western Europe feared a Habsburg take over. France felt herself particularly vulnerable as she was almost entirely surrounded on her land frontiers by countries which were under Habsburg control. To the north-east were the Netherlands, to the east Franche–Comté and to the south-west Spain herself.

*   If the other European powers feared Habsburg domination, the Habsburg rulers felt it a matter of pride that they should not lose any of their patrimony. At all costs, the lands that they had inherited had to be preserved and handed to their successors intact.

However, Charles I had not just acquired territorial power. He had also become Holy Roman Emperor as Charles V. This had brought him the responsibility of defending the Roman Catholic religion both against the threat of Islam and against the growing threat of Protestantism even within the very lands over which he ruled. The importance of this role in defending the Roman Catholic religion against Islam, especially the Ottoman Empire ruled over by the Turks, was to have serious repercussions on the ability of the Habsburgs to defend their lands against other Christian rulers and against the Protestant threat. From the fourteenth century the Ottoman Empire had expanded from Anatolia, into Europe via the Balkans, and into the Middle East via Palestine. In the early sixteenth century, under Suleiman the Magnificent, the Turks took the island of Rhodes. Control of the eastern Mediterranean was then theirs. On land they conquered part of Hungary and also controlled North Africa. On all sides the Habsburgs were therefore to feel the Islamic threat. The safety of their lands as well as defence of the Roman Catholic religion demanded Habsburg action against followers of Islam.

At the same time, the growth of Protestantism forced the Habsburgs to strive for the purity of the faith within their own lands. Protection of that faith was a prime consideration in dealing with the component parts that made up their lands and failure to compromise led to long and costly struggles. As a result, the Habsburgs were involved in almost continuous warfare throughout the sixteenth and early seventeenth centuries.

Defence of their territories and religion required an effective army and navy. The Habsburgs were generally fortunate in this respect. During the reign of Ferdinand and Isabella the 'Great Captain', Gonzalo de Córdoba, had created a professional army based on the infantry. At the core of this army were the Spanish troops who were to dominate warfare in Europe for much of the sixteenth century, under the skilled leadership of such commanders as the Duke of Alba, Don John of Austria and Alexander Farnese, Duke of Parma. Spain also made a major contribution to the navy, with the Netherlands and the Habsburg states in Italy contributing a small number of vessels.

It must be remembered that the Empire was never a Spanish one. Each area felt itself to be of equal importance and to be considered worthy of equal esteem from its ruler. The ruler of the people in each state was their king, their count or their duke. Most were not interested in the wider aspects of his rule. Each part of the Empire had a different history. Each part had developed different methods of government and had different rights and privileges in relation to its ruler. Their only common elements were loyalty to the ruler and loyalty to the Roman Catholic faith.

* In practice, the base of the Empire became Castile, which was to become under Charles I the most loyal and obedient province in the Empire. From the time of Philip II, Madrid became the centre of Habsburg rule and the king was rarely to leave it. Castile alone bore the high cost of the court. Her economic position meant that she could, at least in the sixteenth century, provide much of the financial support needed by the Crown. She was also able until the end of the century to provide much of the manpower needed for the army and navy. The cost to her was high. In return she gained the expensive symbols of royalty – fine buildings, works of art and the elaborate ceremony of the court; and the knowledge that she was at the heart of one of the greatest empires ever known.

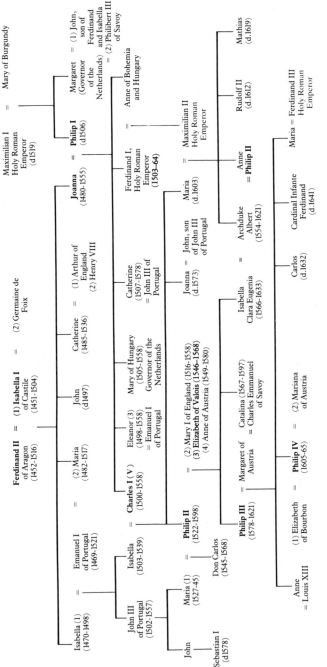

Rulers of Spain 1474–1665

Making notes on '*Introduction, Spain: Rise and Decline, 1474–1643*'

For this chapter make very brief notes. These should enable you to gain a general idea of the main features of Spain in 1450. Think particularly about the ways in which each topic covered contained the seeds of future problems for the government of Spain.

The following headings, questions and activities should help you:

1. The geographical features of Spain and how they influenced her development
2. Early history to the mid-fifteenth century
2.1. The Reconquest
2.2. Aragon's overseas empire
2.3. Reasons for Castile becoming more important than Aragon by the mid-fifteenth century
3. The Cortes
3.1. What was the Crown of Aragon?
3.2. How did the Cortes of Castile differ from those of the Crown of Aragon?
4. Religion
4.1. The three religious groups and their relations with each other before the fifteenth century
4.2. Reasons for growth of hostility of Christians towards Jews and Muslims
4.3. Who were the *conversos* or 'new' Christians'?
5. The 'Monarchy' or Empire
5.1. Draw a map to show details of the extent of the Empire
5.2. The Habsburg connection with Spain
5.3. Who were the enemies of the Habsburgs and why?
5.4. The two main aims of the Habsburgs
5.5. Developments in the army
5.6. How much unity was there within the Empire?
5.7. Reasons for the primacy of Castile in the Empire

CHAPTER 2

Ferdinand and Isabella, 1479–1516

On 19 October 1469, the 18-year-old Isabella, half-sister and heir to the King of Castile, secretly married her cousin, the 17-year-old Ferdinand, son and heir to the King of Aragon. Both countries were suffering from the effects of civil war. In Castile the nobles had been disputing the power of the King since 1464 while Catalonia had revolted against the rule of Ferdinand's father in 1462 and was not to be defeated until ten years later. There was no guarantee, therefore, that either of the two newly-weds would succeed to their respective kingdoms.

This was particularly the case with Isabella whose half-brother, King Henry IV of Castile, had a daughter, Joanna. It was, however, widely believed that Joanna was illegitimate, and Henry had agreed to acknowledge Isabella as his heir. When Henry died in 1474 Isabella proclaimed herself Queen of Castile. At the same time Joanna also claimed the throne. To help her in her claim, Joanna had the support of King Alfonso V of Portugal to whom she became engaged. A War of Succession broke out between the supporters of Joanna and those of Isabella. It took five years for Isabella, with the help of Ferdinand, to gain control of all Castile. Joanna, following the failure of her claim, went into a convent in Portugal, there to remain for the rest of her life 'unmarried and a nun'. In the same year, 1479, Ferdinand's father died. Ferdinand and Isabella were now the rulers of Aragon and Castile respectively.

Ferdinand, though one year younger than his wife, had much more experience of both politics and military affairs. As king he was to prove skilful and pragmatic in his handling of political matters, being described by one contemporary writer as never preaching

> anything except peace and good faith; and he is an enemy of both one and the other, and if he had ever honoured either of them he would have lost either his standing or his state many times over.

In war he was to display personal bravery and a capacity for inspiring those who fought under him. Although he was pious, he was not extreme in religious matters. This could not be said of Isabella, his energetic wife, who was also to be honoured and served loyally by the majority of her subjects.

The two monarchs were king and queen of Aragon and Castile, not of Spain. The union was a personal one. By their marriage contract it was made clear that Isabella alone was the 'rightful heir to these kingdoms of Castile and Leon'. Ferdinand was given little personal power in Castile apart from that allowed him by Isabella. All appointments had to have Isabella's agreement, and Ferdinand had to respect the traditions of Castile. Any children of the marriage had to be educated in Castile. Isabella in her turn was given little say in the running of the kingdom of

Aragon.

In practice the partnership seems to have been successful. Ferdinand and Isabella in general worked closely and in harmony together. The heads of both appeared on seals and coins. The arms of both kingdoms appeared together on banners. Both their initials were engraved on their furniture and personal possessions. Both monarchs signed royal decrees and both were responsible for ecclesiastical and administrative appointments. Isabella also made sure that Ferdinand played an active part in the governing of Castile and much of the conduct of the foreign policy of both Aragon and Castile was left to him. So close was their working relationship that one chronicler of the reign made an imaginary report that 'on such and such a day, the king and queen gave birth to a daughter'.

It was clear from the start that each kingdom was still to be considered as separate from the other. Each was to retain its own form of government, keep its own language (mainly Castilian in Castile and Catalan in the Crown of Aragon), and its own laws and customs. In addition, virtually nothing was done to bring the economics of the two kingdoms into closer union. Trade remained difficult with the continuance of internal customs barriers between the two realms. If a merchant wished to bring his goods across the frontier between Aragon and Castile he would have to pay duties on these goods. Even more divisive was the fact that, once exploration of the New World opened up new markets for goods to and from America, it was only those who lived in Castile who were allowed to participate – much to the annoyance of the experienced Catalan merchants. In comparison the economic unity brought about by improvements to the roads which went across both realms was of little significance.

1 The Conquest of Granada

The marriage at least brought an end to possible conflict between the kingdoms of Aragon and Castile. The monarchs could now give attention to the last non-Christian kingdom in the Iberian peninsula, Granada (see map on page 5). Border warfare had taken place on the frontier between Castile and Granada for many years. Raids and counter raids continued even during periods of truce. In 1481 the capture by Moors of a frontier town in Andalusia gave the two monarchs an excuse for a military campaign against Granada.

Ferdinand and Isabella stressed the importance of the crusading aspect of the war. It was a chance to complete the Reconquest and bring the whole of the Iberian Peninsula under Christian rule, although this idea only took shape as the war progressed. In 1481 the monarchs were only talking of making war 'on the Moors from every direction'. Contemporary letters refer to the war as a crusade and the monarchs as taking 'on the holy expedition with the intention rather to spread abroad the religion of Christ than to increase their earthly empire'. The Pope allowed them to collect the taxes on the clergy usually given for crusades. His gift of a large silver cross was carried by the army throughout the war. The chains of Christian captives freed during the war were hung up in churches 'to be revered by successive generations as the trophies of Christian warfare'.

The war lasted ten years and led to a Christian victory only after a hard and expensive struggle. The end was marked by the capture of the city of Granada in 1492. A number of factors contributed to this eventual victory. Conquest was made easier by the fact that the rulers of Granada were divided among themselves. In addition, little help was received from other Muslim states (particularly those in North Africa). On the Christian side, the nobles of Andalusia, the area of Castile nearest to Granada, played a significant part in the victory. They knew the area well and had experience in dealing with their Moorish opponents. The personal presence of the two monarchs helped encourage their forces. Ferdinand was in charge of the campaign and Isabella made sure that supplies reached the armies. The use of artillery by the Christian forces was crucial, as it enabled them to deal with sieges in weeks rather than months. One Muslim contemporary had no doubt about its importance in at least one campaign:

> the Christian disposed of cannons with which he launched fire-bombs. . . . These projectiles were one of the causes for the abandonment of the places on which they fell.

The war was expensive and under normal circumstances the monarchs would probably have been unable to sustain it for so long. That they could do so was partly due to the grants given by the Pope and the *Hermandad,* the local peace-keeping forces. The Jews also contributed a special levy for the war, and interest free loans were given by many of their other subjects.

In spite of the length and cost of the war, the terms of the treaty which ended it were generous. Moors were allowed to keep their own religion, dress, customs and property. Those who wished to emigrate were able, and even encouraged, to do so. Out of the original half a million Moors in Granada, 100 000 died during the fighting or were enslaved, 200 000 emigrated and about 200 000 remained.

The conquest of Granada was welcomed throughout Christendom. Other rulers in Europe sent their congratulations. The Pope gave Ferdinand and Isabella the title of 'Catholic Monarchs'. 'Will there ever be an age so thankless as will not hold you in eternal gratitude?' wrote one contemporary. The victory had increased the monarchs' prestige among the other countries of Europe. It had assured them of their positions on their thrones. The use of artillery had been considerably developed during the course of the war against the Moors and was to be used in future wars against France. The war had also helped bring some feeling of unity to the peoples of Castile and Aragon. Men had come from all over the two kingdoms to fight together against their common enemy:

1   Who would have thought that the Galician, the proud Asturian and
    the rude inhabitant of the Pyrenees, would be mixing freely with
    Toledans, people of La Mancha, and Andalucians, living together
    in harmony and obedience, like members of one family, speaking
5   the same language and subject to one common discipline.

2 Internal Policies

a) The Establishment of Order in Castile and Aragon

The prestige and security brought to the monarchy by the victory in Granada were enhanced by the peace and order Ferdinand and Isabella secured in their kingdoms.

In the past, some historians have considered that Ferdinand and Isabella were aiming to establish some kind of absolute monarchy in Castile and Aragon. This is unlikely to be true. In their own documents they refer to a 'pre-eminent monarchy'. What this seems to imply is that they aimed to create a strong position for the Crown which would enable them to ensure justice and order in Castile and Aragon, but at the same time they were prepared to respect the rights and customs of the individual kingdoms. One of their first considerations as rulers was therefore the establishment of an effective system of justice and order. They put most effort into achieving this in Castile which, from early in the reign, seems to have been considered by both monarchs as the more important of their kingdoms.

Ferdinand and Isabella partly created order by their personal presence. As monarchs, they were constantly on the move, going from one part of their kingdoms to another. There was no fixed court. Their officials and advisers travelled with them. This usually enabled them to be in any place where there might be problems. They could then arbitrate in disputes, hear lawsuits and deal personally with revolts.

Another means of control was through the *Hermandades*. These were brotherhoods which had been used in several Castilian towns in the past to keep the peace. In 1476 a *Santa Hermandad* was set up in every place with more than fifty inhabitants. They were controlled directly by the Crown. Their main task was to police the towns and villages, including the neighbouring countryside. The *Hermandades* also tried people for certain crimes such as robbery, murder and arson. The punishments they could inflict were often severe and included mutilation and death. Even for this period, the *Hermandades* were regarded as harsh:

1   . . . justice was so severe that it appeared to be cruelty, but it was
    necessary because all the kingdoms had not been pacified, nor had
    the dominions of tyrants and haughty men been abased. And

because of this there was much veritable butchery of men with the
5   cutting off of feet, hands, shoulders, and heads, without sparing or
disguising the rigours of justice.

By the time the *Hermandades* were disbanded in 1498 they had done
much to ensure order in the localities in Castile. Attempts to extend a
similar system to Aragon were not, however, successful.

The Catholic Monarchs made their presence felt in many of the towns
in Castile. They continued the policy, started in the fourteenth century,
of sending out *corregidores* (or civil governors) to collect taxes, to report to
the Crown on the state of affairs in the area, and to ensure that royal
jurisdiction was not interfered with by members of the Church or the
nobility. Other royal officials were sent out to check on the work that the
corregidores were doing.

Many of the disturbances in the past had been due to the civil wars in
which the nobles had played a major part. Measures were therefore taken
to control these nobles. Troublesome ones were arrested, their castles
were burnt and much of their property was taken from them. The Crown
also tried to recover rights and lands it had previously lost. At the Cortes
of Toledo in 1480, almost all royal lands lost since 1464 were returned to
the Crown. However, the many lands lost before that date were to be
kept by the nobles. Compensation was given for any lands reclaimed by
the Crown in the form of lands conquered in Granada. The important
coastal cities of Cartagena and Cadiz, which helped control the southern
coast, were taken under royal control, and the nobles who had previously
held them were granted other towns as compensation. In addition,
nobles were forbidden to make private war or to build new castles.

At the same time, steps were taken to try to ensure the support of the
nobles. Ferdinand and Isabella encouraged the titled nobility to spend
time at their court. Opportunities were given to nobles to serve in foreign
wars. Support for the Crown led to rewards, and many new titles were
created. The Crown also supported the efforts of nobles to remain
economically viable. The nobles were encouraged to use the *mayorazgo*,
or entail, which forbade sales or division of land. This meant that
property and land could descend from one generation to another without
being divided into smaller pieces and this helped prevent disputes within
families.

The Crown extended its hold over the military orders in Castile. These
were orders of chivalry made up of knights bound by religious vows. The
three in Castile – Santiago, Calatrava, and Alcantara – were a group of
importance. They owned large estates and received much wealth which
made them extremely powerful. Isabella was determined, therefore, that
they should come under the control of the Crown. This was achieved
when Ferdinand became Grand Master of each of the orders. The Crown
thus increased its income considerably. In 1489 a council was set up
specifically for the administration of the orders.

The nobles, particularly those in Castile, were prepared to accept the rule of the two monarchs. A contemporary view was that,

1   they kept a great household and court, accompanied by Grandees and leading barons, whom they honoured and elevated according to the quality of their degree, keeping them occupied in ways wherein they could be of service, and when occasion arose, mindful
5   to serve in the government of the kingdom and the Royal Council. The monarchs were most careful to place men of prudence and ability to serve, even though such were of the middling sort rather than great men from the noblest houses.

b) Administration

Many of these 'middling sort' were to sit on the various councils which made up the main central administration of the government. The main council was the Royal Council of Castile. This consisted of five parts or chambers: that which discussed foreign policy, that which acted as the main court of justice, that which dealt with the *Hermandades,* that for finance, and, finally, the group of nobles and *letrados,* 'people mid-way between the great and the small whose profession was to study law', from Aragon, Catalonia, Majorca, Valencia and Sicily. In 1494, this last became a council in its own right – the Council of Aragon. Further new councils were formed: in 1483 that of the Supreme Inquisition and in 1489 that of the Council of Orders (to deal with the military orders).

There was nothing essentially new about this system. The conciliar system had been established early in the century in Castile. What the two monarchs did was to increase the number of councils to meet their growing responsibilities. The use of *letrados* can also be traced to before the reign of Isabella, though their numbers increased during her reign. By 1493 all members of the Royal Council had to be *letrados*, with at least ten years' study of law at university.

Attempts were also made by Ferdinand and Isabella to increase their control over justice. This was difficult even in Castile because of the local rights and powers of the nobles and the Church. In 1489 ordinances were issued establishing a permanent court at Valladolid. Further permanent courts were later established in Granada, Santiago de Compostela, and Seville. The former two were considered the most important and appeals from these went to the Council of Castile, the highest court. Both criminal and civil cases were tried by the courts. Attempts were made to ensure that similar laws were in operation over all Castile. Collections of all the late medieval law codes and the *pragmaticas* of the Catholic Monarchs were published. The *pragmaticas* were laws which the two monarchs had issued without going through the Cortes of Castile but which still had to be obeyed by the inhabitants of Castile.

c) Finance

An important means by which Ferdinand and Isabella were able to secure their position was by increasing their income. At the beginning of the reign obtaining finance was a considerable problem. Not only was Spain a poor country in itself but the civil wars of the 1470s had made the normal income from taxes difficult to collect. In 1477 this income stood at 27 million *maravedís*. Most of it was raised from the *alcabala*, or sales tax, and the rest from such sources as customs. Instead of having official tax collectors, Ferdinand and Isabella accepted lump sum payments from tax farmers, who paid for the right to collect the taxes.

Money was needed mainly for the court, the army and the ambassadors who were a vital part of the monarchy's foreign policy. Ferdinand and Isabella did not pay out lavish sums on a fixed court and did not spend excessively on themselves. However a certain amount of expenditure was necessary if the monarchs were to be seen as greater in status than their subjects. In addition, large sums had to be spent on the upkeep of royal residences and on foreign ambassadors. In the last ten years of Isabella's reign, in Castile 75 million *maravedís* were spent on ambassadors. From 1482 onwards there was also much more involvement in warfare. The cost of the royal militia and ordnance (military equipment) consequently rose from 20 million in that year to 80 million in 1504. The wars fought against France in Italy and in Roussillon (see page 24) cost an exorbitant amount. Ferdinand's foreign policy also involved expensive royal marriage alliances.

The cost for all this could not be met from ordinary income. The finance for the war in Granada had been largely met from Church sources, but other methods still had to be found for the rest. Collection of taxes became more efficient. Revenue from customs duties increased as trade improved. However, it was in the extraordinary sources of income that the real change came. These increased by 66 per cent compared with earlier reigns. The military orders, the *Hermandad*, papal grants, and loans all contributed much. But most came from the large sums of money voted by the Castilian Cortes in special taxes, amounting to almost 300 million *maravedís* in the years 1500–1504 alone.

d) Religious Policies

Desire for money has been suggested as one of the reasons for the introduction of the Inquisition into Spain and for the expulsion of the Jews. The Inquisition was an institution introduced initially to deal with the *conversos* (Jews converted to Christianity). Wealthy *conversos* might have large estates which would be confiscated if their owner was found guilty by the Inquisition, 'this Inquisition is as much to take the *conversos*'s estates as to exalt the faith . . . goods are heretics', declared one *converso*. Certainly some large sums were raised in this way but the costs of running the Inquisition were also high and it is unlikely that the Crown made much, if any, financial gain out of it. In some cities persecution of *conversos* caused serious economic damage by removing key people, especially in the financing of trade and industry, and thereby led to a decline in royal income. Ferdinand seemed well aware of the harm that it could do to Crown income in this letter sent in 1484:

1　Before We decided to allow this Inquisition to act in any city . . . We had considered all the harm that might result to our royal rights and revenues. But, since Our firm intention and zeal is to place the service of Our Lord God before Our own . . . We wish that this
5　should be done, all other interests put aside.

The most likely reason for the introduction of the Inquisition was therefore concern for the Christian religion.

Much evidence had come to the Crown that the *conversos*, or 'new Christians' as they were often called, were not all genuine converts and that they still secretly practised their former Jewish faith and kept at least some of their Jewish customs. It was commonly held that 'hardly any are true Christians, as is well known in all Spain'. There was probably some truth in this. Many Jews had been forcibly converted in previous years in both kingdoms. In addition, most of them had been given no adequate Christian teaching. Fear of the *conversos* was often mingled with resentment and envy, for many of them were wealthy and they, or their descendants, held important positions in the two kingdoms.

A papal inquisition had existed since the thirteenth century in Aragon but had not operated for many years. The new Inquisition was to be completely under the control of the monarchs and to be independent of both pope and bishops. Appointments to the Inquisition were made by the Crown and its accounts closely supervised. In this way, Ferdinand and Isabella were able to gain more control over the Church in Spain. The new Inquisition was set up in 1478 and extended, with difficulty, owing to much opposition, to Aragon six years later.

In the early years the Inquisition put many people to death. In Seville alone between 1480 and 1488 over 700 *conversos* were burned and many thousands received other punishments. In total between 1483 and 1498 approximately 2000 people were burned. The Inquisition was justly feared by the *conversos*. Its courts worked in secret and had great power. No one could appeal against their verdicts. The accusors were not named. Those found guilty could be fined, lose their property, be imprisoned or burnt at the stake in public. To inspire a 'horror of heresy' many of the guilty were made to walk in the *autos de fe*. These were the ceremonies at which accused persons were sentenced by the Inquisition. The burning of any heretics took place after such ceremonies.

The role of the Inquisition gradually extended beyond dealing with *conversos*. It came to be concerned with matters involving people's daily lives. People could find themselves brought before its courts over what they had said or written, for sexual misconduct, usury (charging high interest rates on loans of money), witchcraft or blasphemy.

On the other hand, one must not go as far as some historians in the past who have suggested that the Inquisition was like the secret police in some twentieth-century totalitarian states. The numbers executed by the Inquisition in its first century of operation were, for example, much smaller than the numbers killed for witchcraft in Germany during the seventeenth century.

The Inquisition brought to light many more cases of Judaism among the *conversos* than the Crown expected. The two monarchs decided that stronger measures would have to be employed if the contagion of Judaism was to be halted and the souls of *conversos* saved. The remedy decided on was one that had been suggested in the past – the expulsion of all the Jews from the two kingdoms.

Violence and hatred of the Jews had increased during the reign of Isabella and Ferdinand. The following comment about the Jews by a contemporary Christian is typical:

> All their work was to multiply and increase. . . . They never wanted to take manual work, ploughing or digging or walking the fields with the herds . . . but only jobs in the towns, so as to sit around making money without doing much work.

What the writer fails to mention is the problems the Jews had in being accepted into any jobs other than those involving finance. Even a generally enlightened writer considered the Jews

> obscene, detestable, vile, execrable . . . to be ostracized from all human contact. . . . My sovereigns were the wisest of men to think of exterminating that despicable and infected herd.

The measures taken by the two monarchs had encouraged anti-Judaism among the 'old' 'Christians. Ferdinand and Isabella had implemented the decrees which ordered the walling off of Jewish sections of towns from Christian sections. The Jews were made to wear distinctive yellow badges in some parts of the kingdoms. Further laws made it possible for Christians to refuse to pay any debts they owed to Jews.

The policy of expulsion started in 1482. It became official policy in March 1492 when a decree was issued stating that Jews must become Christians or leave the two kingdoms within four months. Estimates of how many left as a result vary considerably – possibly as many as 150 000 from Castile and 15 000 from Aragon. An anti-Jewish writer of the time captures the atmosphere of their exit:

1   They went out from the lands of their births, boys and adults, old men and children, on foot, and riding on donkeys and other beasts and in wagons. . . . They went by the roads and fields with much labour and ill-fortune, some collapsing, others getting up, some

5 dying, others giving birth, others falling ill, so that there was no
Christian who was not sorry for them . . . the rabbis were encou-
raging them and making the women and boys sing and beat drums
and tambourines to enliven the people. And so they went out of
Castile.

The following personal reminiscence by an exile is in a somewhat
different tone:

1 I have personally witnessed the Jewish expulsion from Spain,
Sicily, and Sardinia in 1492 and again from Portugal in 1497. . . .
We reached Africa (from Portugal) after having been taken captive
two times. May God, in His grace and mercy, reward me and my
5 son, that we may continue to the end to serve His blessed Name.

Most Jews who went into exile lost a considerable number of their
possessions and much of any wealth they had. With them, however, went
their valuable economic skills. The Sultan of Turkey is reported as
saying that he 'marvelled greatly at expelling the Jews from Spain since
this was to expel its wealth'. In this respect he may have exaggerated.
Many of the *conversos* took the places of the Jews who left so that the
effect, particularly on the economy, may not have been so serious as was
once thought by historians.

Hatred by 'old' Christians for the Muslims was nowhere near as violent
as that experienced by Jews and *conversos*. In Aragon there were many
Muslims to be found, mainly working on the estates of the nobles. In
Castile there were fewer originally, but the conquest of Granada led to
many more Muslims coming under the rule of Ferdinand and Isabella.
Two major problems then confronted the monarchs. The first was that of
security. There were always fears that Muslims would ally with the
enemies of Spain in any invasion of the country. To the north-east,
beyond the Pyrenees, were the French and to the south, the Muslims of
North Africa. In the Mediterranean the Turks were a power to be feared.
Secondly, there was, at least on Isabella's part, a genuine desire to see the
spread of Christianity among the Muslims.

After the conquest of Granada, Hernando de Talavera was made
Archbishop. He worked patiently and sincerely to try to convert the
Muslims. However, many in Castile thought that this policy brought
change too slowly. Cisneros, Archbishop of Toledo, therefore pressed
Isabella to pursue a more determined policy to try to convert as many of
the Muslims as possible. Thousands became Christians, though probably through fear and not from any real change of faith. In addition a
heavy tax was levied on the Muslims in 1495 and again in 1499. These
measures made the position of many Muslims intolerable and it is hardly
surprising that in 1499 a revolt broke out against Castilian rule. This was
the excuse needed by Isabella. A force was sent into Granada, and the
revolt was put down in three months of bitter fighting. A campaign

ensued to ensure that all Muslims were now converted. Permission was given for them to emigrate if they preferred this to conversion, but difficulties were put in their way, including having to leave behind their children, so few left. Those who remained were now known as *Moriscos* (Christian Moors). The Muslims in Castile were given the choice in 1502 of either becoming Christians or leaving. Again, most remained. Muslims were now only to be found in the kingdom of Aragon and Ferdinand resisted any attempt to extend this policy of conversion or expulsion there.

The treatment of the Jews, the Muslims and the *conversos* were the three major elements in Ferdinand's and Isabella's religious policies which were in general new. Their attempts to reform the Christian clergy and to gain more control over the Spanish Church were much more a continuation of the policies of previous years.

Control of the Church would help the two monarchs in their task of bringing peace to the kingdoms and enable them to prevent bishops from acting like warlike nobles. Ferdinand and Isabella succeeded in gaining the Pope's agreement to their making all the Church appointments in Granada and the Canaries. In America, they not only held this right but could also sack clergy and raise taxes from the Church. Within Spain they managed to secure some degree of nomination rights over the appointment of bishops. They also prevented most appeals going to the Pope. Less successful, however, were their attempts to reduce the juridical rights of the clergy. This meant that the clergy could continue to insist on being tried for any crime before a Church court. This usually meant that, if found guilty, they would receive a much lighter sentence than in a royal court.

The crown used its ability to appoint bishops to try to ensure that those appointed would set a good example. The new appointments tended to be of non-noble origin and so less likely to engage in war than many of the bishops from noble backgrounds. New colleges were set up especially for the education of the higher clergy.

These new bishops seem to have been concerned to ensure that measures were taken against clergy for living with women, for not residing at the post to which they were appointed (non-residence), and for wearing unsuitable dress. But the effects seem to have been limited. In 1500 Isabella wrote to one bishop pointing out that in his diocese

the greater part of the clergy are said to be and are in concubinage publicly, and if Our justice intervenes to punish them they revolt.

Clergy in another diocese had to be told

not to gamble or fight bulls or sing or dance in public.

Complaints were still being made in 1511 of clergy who had obtained their positions by every means apart from their own merit! There were similar problems with members of the religious orders and these also proved difficult to overcome.

3 The Beginning of the Overseas Empire

With hindsight, the Spanish of the mid-sixteenth century would look back and describe the 'discovery' of America as being 'the greatest event since the creation of the world'. At the time, however, it was considered as the least of Ferdinand's and Isabella's achievements. By the end of the reign little had been found apart from a small amount of gold and the natives who lived there.

Spanish involvement had started with the first voyage of the Italian sailor, Christopher Columbus. Rejected by the other major sea-faring nations of the time, Portugal, France and England, he had finally persuaded Isabella to support him in his venture to find a route west across the Atlantic to the Spice Islands of the East Indies. In 1492, sailing from Palus with three ships,, he reached the Bahamas by the end of the year and from there went on to Hispaniola. Columbus thought he had reached the East Indies and the valuable Spice Islands on his voyage west. This was the exciting news he took back to Spain. Three further voyages were undertaken by Columbus who discovered more of the West Indian Islands and part of the mainland of South America. Gradually it became clear that what had been found were new lands to the Europeans. Columbus had discovered the sea route to and from the continent which came to be known as America.

Ferdinand and Isabella wished to ensure their position with regard to their new possessions, particularly as they feared that the Portuguese, the chief sea-faring nation in Europe at the time, might put in their own claims. The Pope, Alexander VI, himself a Spaniard and therefore likely to be sympathetic to the Spanish cause, issued a number of papal bulls. The most important was the *Inter Caetara* of 1493 which confirmed the Spanish rights to the new lands in South America. In the Treaty of Tordesillas, made with the Portuguese the following year, Spain agreed to move the line which marked Spanish territory further west. This change was thought to be relatively unimportant at the time but it meant that when Brazil was later explored, it became part of the Portuguese rather than the Spanish Empire.

4 Foreign Policy

The 'discoveries' of America and its consequent rewards had gone to Castile. Aragon had played little part in them. In foreign policy, however, a much closer partnership could be found between the two kingdoms. Here it was Aragon's lead which was in general followed, with the finances and resources coming mainly from Castile.

* The enmity between Spain and Portugal at the beginning of

Ferdinand's and Isabella's reign over the succession to the throne of Castile was to continue over ownership of the Canary Islands. In the Treaty of Alcaçovas (1479) Portugal gave up her claims to the islands, and by the 1490s the major islands had been conquered and made part of the Crown of Castile. Relations after this became more friendly. Isabella, the eldest daughter of the two monarchs, was married first to the heir of the King of Portugal and then, on his death, to the new king. On her own death in childbirth her husband was to marry her sister, Maria. The peace cemented by these marriages was to prove long lasting. It meant that Ferdinand and Isabella could turn their attention elsewhere without fearing a possible invasion of Castile from Portugal.

* Relations with France were difficult for most of the reign. There had for long been disputes between France and the Crown of Aragon over two of Catalonia's northern provinces, Cerdagne and Roussillon. These had been occupied by France since 1462. An attempt to recover them by force failed. However, by the early 1490s France's attention was directed towards Italy and she was prepared to give up both Cerdagne and Roussillon to Spain by the Treaty of Barcelona (1493).

The French invasion of Italy in 1494 was to lead to renewed conflict between France and Spain. The French forces quickly reached as far south as Naples (see map page 35), meeting little resistance on the way. In Naples the ruler was Ferdinand's illegitimate cousin and brother-in-law, King Ferrante. Ferrante's position was weak at the time of the invasion and he could not rely on help from either his own nobles or Ferdinand.

Already in 1493 some contemporaries foresaw that Spain would wish to take possession of Naples:

> the whole of Italy is in conspiracy against your state (Naples) . . .
> France is on the way. Spain holds you in its hand, awaiting its time.

This suggestion that Ferdinand might wish to take over Naples for himself seems supported by his instructions to his ambassador in France:

1   the war of Naples touches only [our] own interests. Naples had
    previously been a part of the Crown of Aragon. Therefore it fell to
    them [the rulers of Aragon] to reconquer the kingdom of Naples
    and that of Granada, which were both usurped from their
5   predecessors.

The reasons given to other states for Ferdinand's involvement in Naples were different. In January 1496 the monarchs wrote to their ambassador in England:

1   You know already that this war we have with the King of France is
    not for any interest of our own but to aid the Pope in order that the
    King of France may restore what he had taken from the Church by
    force; and he presumes to occupy and make war on the kingdom of

5 Naples which is feudatory of the Church and as all Christian
  princes must defend the Pope and the lands of the Church, we, in
  order to fulfil that obligation and obey the Pope's commands . . .
  opened this war with France.

In a letter to his viceroy in Sicily Ferdinand wrote in 1495:

> We, seeing the war in all Italy, and because We have heard that the
> Turk has a great fleet prepared, are sending a fleet and troops.

In the main it is likely that it was his concern about France which
governed Ferdinand's actions. He would not wish France to be in control
of Naples and so be a danger to Spanish policy in the central Mediterranean area.

Ferdinand did not act alone against France. In 1495 he joined with the
Empire, represented by Maximilian of Austria, the Papacy and some
other Italian states against the French. The Spanish forces were under
the 'Great Captain', Gonzalo de Córdoba. They employed new methods
and the artillery, which had been so successful in Granada, to expel the
French from Naples in two campaigns (1495–1497 and 1501–1504). In
1504 France recognised Spanish control over Naples, and it became part
of the Crown of Aragon.

Naples was a valuable acquisition to Spain. She was important geogra-
phically, seated as she was in the central area of the Mediterranean. Her
grain supplies were a considerable gain as was her revenue. However, she
also brought further commitments to Spain. Spain's toehold in Italy
through Naples was to lead to further military and diplomatic warfare
against France. It also extended the length of the Spanish frontier in the
Mediterranean which would need to be defended against the Turks.

Further conquests took place in the Iberian Peninsula itself. Navarre
and Portugal were, after the fall of Granada, the only two parts of the
peninsula not under the rule of Ferdinand and Isabella. Though small,
Navarre was important because of its geographical position between
France and Spain. Control of Navarre by France could give her a base
from which to invade Spain. A further difficulty was that part of Navarre
lay in France and was therefore subject to the French King. Problems
over the control of Navarre had persisted over many decades. A disputed
succession to its throne led to Ferdinand's invasion of 1512. All the
fortresses surrendered within a few weeks and Navarre became part of
the Crown of Castile.

* The interests of Aragon in the Mediterranean brought her into
contact with the Muslims. Considerations of defence were uppermost in
Ferdinand's mind but he also expressed an interest in a crusade against
the Turks on several occasions, 'from my youth I was always very
inclined to war against infidels and it is the thing in which I receive most
delight and pleasure'. Isabella's religious views and the feelings of many
Castilians, heirs to the Reconquest, also led to a desire to fight the Turks.

In 1479–1480 Spain assisted the Knights Hospitallers when the island of Rhodes was besieged by the Turks. A year later Spain, along with Portugal, helped Naples against a Turkish invasion.

In the 1490s Ferdinand's attention was drawn to North Africa. Chief among the reasons for this were the questions of religion and security. To act against the Moors of North Africa would also be to act against the main rival religious faith to Christianity and continue the Reconquest. It would also help prevent support being given to the Muslim population in Spain after the conquest of Granada. Several cities along the North African coast were taken in the early years of the sixteenth century. The most important of these were Oran, Bougie and Tripoli. Algiers became a vassal city, which meant it owed allegiance to Spain. However, an attempt to take Djerba, off Tunisia, failed, and the conquests made were only held with difficulty for the rest of Ferdinand's reign, particularly after his interest turned towards Italy.

Ferdinand's foreign policy was aided and supported by the marriage alliances made by members of his family. Apart from the marriage of his daughter Isabella with the ruler of Portugal, close links were also formed with the Habsburgs. In 1496 the son and heir of the Holy Roman Emperor, Philip, married Ferdinand's daughter Joanna. It was from this marriage that was to be born the future Emperor Charles V (Charles I of Spain). The following year Ferdinand's son and heir, John, married Margaret, daughter of the Holy Roman Emperor. Alliances with England were cemented in 1489, in the Treaty of Medina del Campo, by the proposed marriage of another of Ferdinand's daughters, Catherine, to the English heir to the throne, Arthur. When Arthur died it was proposed that Catherine should marry the new heir, the future Henry VIII. This marriage took place in 1509. Ferdinand's own second marriage, to the King of France's niece, Germaine de Foix, took place in 1506, when he was looking for French help against his son-in-law, Philip.

* Another arm to Ferdinand's foreign policy was the use of ambassadors. Here new methods were introduced. Ferdinand was the first European monarch, apart from the rulers of the Italian states, regularly to use resident ambassadors. Before then ambassadors and agents had been used on a temporary basis, for a specific purpose. By the 1490s Spain had resident ambassadors in England, the Papal States (Rome), Burgundy, the Holy Roman Empire and Venice, the states usually allied to Spain. The ambassador could negotiate on behalf of the Spanish Crown, discover relevant information about the country in which he was stationed, and present the Spanish position on any issue to the native ruler.

By the end of his reign, Ferdinand had considerable achievements to his name in foreign policy. His official historian was able to say:

1   For now, who does not see, that, although the title of the empire is

in Germany, its real power is held by the Spanish Kings, who, lords
of a great part of Italy and of the islands of the Mediterranean, carry
war to Africa and send their fleets, following the course of the stars,
5   to the islands of the Indians and the New World, joining the east to
the western limit of Spain and Africa?

There were good reasons for Ferdinand to congratulate himself. Spain's
ambassadors were skilful and adroit at achieving success by diplomacy as
in the recovery of Roussillon and Cerdagne from France. Ferdinand's
army and its equipment was on its way to becoming the most feared
fighting force in Western Europe. The territories held by Castile and
Aragon had increased considerably. Granada, Naples, Navarre, towns
along the North African coast, the Canaries and America.

But already, some signs of future problems were apparent. There was
difficulty in finding enough money to maintain the new conquests, and it
was becoming obvious that in having so many interests outside Spain, it
was impossible to concentrate on any one of them properly. It is interesting to speculate on what might have been accomplished in North
Africa, for example, if attention had not been directed to Italy.

5 Conclusion

a) The Closing Years of the Reign

Isabella died in 1504 worn out by the exertions of her travels and the loss
of so many of her children and grandchildren, in particular, her only son
John, and her favourite daughter, Isabella, Queen of Portugal. The
fragile links that bound Aragon and Castile together were now threat-
ened. Isabella's will left Castile to her eldest surviving daughter, Joanna.
Joanna had already shown signs of mental instability and it was laid down
in the will that 'in her absence, or if she proved unwilling or unable to
govern' Ferdinand was to act as regent. In this way it was hoped that
Ferdinand would keep some control over Castile and that too much
power would not fall into the hands of Joanna's husband, Philip of
Austria. Philip resented this. In addition many of the Castilian nobles did
not wish Ferdinand to have any more say in their country. When Philip
and Joanna arrived in Castile from Burgundy, Ferdinand went to meet
them. After a hostile discussion, he agreed to give up the government of
Castile to Philip and returned to Aragon. Ferdinand married Germaine
de Foix in 1506 and probably hoped for an heir, which would prevent
Aragon also coming under the rule of Joanna. It seemed that the two
kingdoms would again separate, the one to be ruled by Joanna, the other
by the heir of Ferdinand and Germaine.

Chance was to decree otherwise. In 1506 Philip died unexpectedly and
Joanna's mind went completely as a result of the loss of the faithless man

she had loved so much. She refused to let his coffin be buried and took it with her to the fortress of Tordesillas. Cardinal Cisneros became Regent briefly, and in accordance with Isabella's will, invited Ferdinand to return to Castile. Ferdinand's own hopes of a male heir were unrealised. A son was indeed born to Germaine in 1509 but only survived a few hours.

Ferdinand spent most of the remaining years of his life in Castile. In 1516 he himself died. Cisneros became Regent again, but this time on behalf of Charles, son of Joanna and Philip.

b) Did Ferdinand and Isabella create a united Spain?

A major question about the reign of Ferdinand and Isabella which has exercised historians of this period is how far the two monarchs unified Spain under their rule. There are several possible ways of approaching this issue. Was there some formal agreement between the two crowns which made them one? Were there institutions or organisations which were common to all the kingdoms? Or was there a vaguer type of unity, some feeling of oneness involving those who lived in Castile and Aragon?

One can quickly dispose of the first of these possible criteria. At no time was there any agreement that Ferdinand and Isabella were rulers over a kingdom of Spain. It was not in fact until the end of the seventeenth century that the monarchs of Castile and Aragon started to refer to themselves as kings 'of the Spains', and even then there was no legal basis for the title. The marriage contract also showed the determination of the two kingdoms, particularly Castile, to maintain their separate identities.

The second criterion needs more detailed investigation, but here again there are few signs of even an intention on the part of Ferdinand and Isabella to bring unity. The Inquisition was introduced into both Castile and Aragon and the Council of the Inquisition was responsible for its activities in the two realms. Apart from this council, however, there was no important common council which looked at affairs in both Castile and Aragon together. As Ferdinand spent most of his time in Castile, he had to decide on how Aragon should be governed in his absence. The solution was not a joint council for the two kingdoms but a separate council set up to advise solely on the affairs of Aragon. Other organisations such as the *Hermandades* were established only in Castile. No one body was formed to deal with foreign policy. When additional territory was acquired it was assigned to either Castile or Aragon. Thus Castile obtained the Indies and to Aragon went Naples. Almost nothing was done to bring economic union.

There is more evidence to be found if signs of informal unity are sought. Ferdinand and Isabella certainly worked closely together on a personal level. The two monarchs acted together over foreign policy, in which Castilian troops and money supported generally traditional Aragonese aims.

People from many parts of the two realms fought together, as in the war to conquer Granada. There was usually a common attitude on religious matters. In both realms the Jews were expelled. However, it was only in Castile that the Muslims were given the choice of conversion or expulsion. Castilian gradually became the dominant language. But one must not overstate the situation. Many in the non-Castilian kingdoms feared that union with Castile meant losing their distinct identities and tried to ensure it did not happen. Many resented the Castilians who received the majority of the rewards and offices that the union of the two realms brought. Finally, it must be remembered that there was a real possibility that, after the death of Isabella, the two kingdoms would again go their separate ways.

Making notes on 'Ferdinand and Isabella'

In making notes on this chapter, always keep two sets of questions in mind. How far were the actions of Ferdinand and Isabella new, or were they a continuation of what had happened before their reigns? Did their actions and policies result in Spanish unity or did they not?

The following headings and sub-headings should provide a suitable framework for your notes:
1.   The uniting of Castile and Aragon under Ferdinand and Isabella
1.1.   Their marriage
1.2.   The war of succession
1.3.   The marriage contract
1.4.   How far the economies of the two kingdoms were brought together
2.   The conquest of Granada (especially why it took place and the results)
3.   Internal policies
3.1.   Establishment of order (aims, personal involvement, *Hermandades*, use of *corregidores* in towns, treatment of nobles, military orders)
3.2.   Administration (conciliar system, type of people who sat on the councils, organisation of justice)
3.3.   Finance (problems at beginning of reign, the ways in which the two monarchs obtained money)
3.4.   Religious policies (Inquisition, expulsion of the Jews, the rising of the Muslims in Granada, control over Church, reforms in the Church); for each of these, give both the reasons for the policy and its results
4.   The beginning of the Overseas Empire
4.1.   Columbus's voyages
4.2.   *Inter Caetara* 1493
4.3.   Treaty of Tordesillas 1494

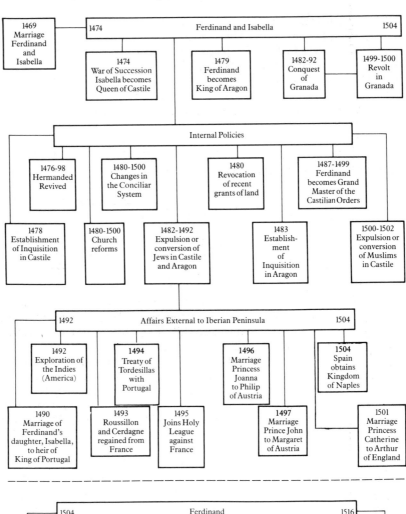

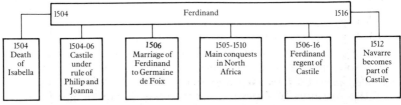

Summary – Spain, 1469–1516

5.   Foreign policy
5.1. Portugal
5.2. Extension of the Empire (Naples, Navarre)
5.3. Conflict with the Moors of North Africa
5.4. Use of ambassadors
5.5. Assessment of Ferdinand's achievements in foreign policy
6.   Conclusion. Did Ferdinand and Isabella unify Spain?

Answering essay questions on 'Ferdinand and Isabella'

Most of the essay questions you will meet on Ferdinand and Isabella will focus on how far the two monarchs unified Spain:

> 'How far did the marriage of Ferdinand and Isabella unify Spain?'
> 'What degree of unity did Ferdinand and Isabella bring to Spain?'
> ' "The unity of Spain under Ferdinand and Isabella was based on religion". Discuss.'

Such questions cannot be answered by a chronological narrative of the reign. You should make a list of the factors that will need to be included. Use the note headings to help you do this. The list will probably include such topics as personal, religion, economics, justice, administration and foreign policy. For each of the factors you have mentioned, list the examples you might use to show how far unity was achieved. Thus for personal, you would probably include something on the ability of Ferdinand and Isabella to work well together. Your essay will then deal with the factors one by one. How would you decide on the order in which to deal with the factors?

The third question given above is a quotation followed by the word discuss. You must not be fooled into thinking that you should concentrate solely on the word 'religion' included in the question. You would be expected to bring in all the other important factors as well. Your answer would therefore need to start with the subject of religion, but would then go on to deal with the other factors.

All the questions ask you to comment on the *relative* importance of each factor. This means that you must comment on how significant a contribution to the unity of Spain under Ferdinand and Isabella was made by *each* factor that you mention.

There might also be questions on how important Spain had become under the rule of Ferdinand and Isabella:

> 'Discuss the strengths and weaknesses of Spain in 1516.'

Make a list of what you consider to be the strengths of Spain in 1516. Consider how far you think that each of the points mentioned is a strength, to whom and why? Is there perhaps any 'weakness' in the 'strength' you mention? Number each point in order of the greatest to the least strength, and in your essay deal with the most important first.

Make a similar list for the weaknesses. This time try to find any strengths in the weakness. For example the powers of the Cortes of the Crown of Aragon might be considered a weakness to the monarch but a strength to those who sat in the Cortes.

You should now be in a position to tackle another very similar essay:

'How far did Spain become a great power by 1516?'

Would you include any different information or comment in an answer to this question?

Source-based questions on 'Ferdinand and Isabella'

1   The Inquisition
Read the extracts on pages 18–19 carefully.
a)   In what ways do these two extracts agree and in what ways do they differ from each other?
b)   Do you regard the authors of the two extracts as impartial authorities? Give reasons for your answer.
c)   How persuasive do you find the tone of these lines from Ferdinand's letter?
d)   Using these documents and your own knowledge explain the reasons for the establishment of the Inquisition by Ferdinand and Isabella.

2   The expulsion of the Jews
Read the extracts on pages 20–21 carefully and answer the following questions:
a)   How far do these extracts explain the dislike of the Christians for the Jews?
b)   Comment on how persuasive or otherwise you find the tone and language of each of the four extracts. Which do you find the most believable? Give reasons for your answer.

3   Foreign Policy
Read the extracts on pages 24–25 carefully and answer the following questions:
a)   What does each of the extracts indicate about the reasons for Ferdinand's interest in Naples?
b)   Explain why you think Ferdinand himself gives two different reasons for his involvement in Naples.
c)   Making use of your own knowledge as well as these extracts, explain why Ferdinand became involved in the affairs of Naples.

CHAPTER 3

Charles I, 1516–56

The new ruler of Spain was a stranger to the country. Charles was a Burgundian and a Habsburg. His Burgundian lands consisted of the Netherlands, Luxembourg and the part of Burgundy known as Franche-Comté (see map on page 35). Charles was born in February 1500 in the rich trading city of Ghent in the Netherlands, and six years later he became ruler of Burgundy on the death of his father, Philip. It was through his father that Charles was a member of the Habsburg family. Charles was the second child of the marriage of Joanna, second daughter of Queen Isabella and King Ferdinand, with Philip I, son of the Emperor Maximilian, head of the Habsburg family. He was also heir to the Habsburg estates of Austria, the Tyrol and parts of southern Germany.

After his father's death his mother remained in Spain, so Charles was brought up with three of his sisters in the loving care of his aunt, the archduchess Margaret of Austria. His education was that of a Burgundian prince. His chief tutor was Adrian of Utrecht, later to be a regent and one of his most important advisers in Spain. As Charles was heir to the Netherlands, Adrian was likely to have emphasised the history of his family to him, and to have instilled in him the dream of reclaiming the original heart of the Burgundian lands, the duchy of Burgundy, which had been lost to France in the previous century. Even his name must have reminded him of his brave and warlike great-grandfather, Charles the Bold, Duke of Burgundy, who was killed in battle in 1477. The life Charles would have grown used to was one of luxury, of expensive clothes and works of art, of hunting and jousting, banquets and music – all the culture and festivities which were such an important feature of the Burgundian court.

Following the death of his grandfather, Ferdinand, in March 1516, Charles was proclaimed King of Aragon, and King of Castile jointly with his mother, Joanna. However it was not until September 1517 that he left for Spain to receive oaths of allegiance from his new kingdoms. To some historians, mainly those writing some years ago, and to some contemporary Spaniards, this showed his reluctance to take up his new position. The view of most modern historians is different. Charles could not afford to leave the Netherlands when there was a possibility of it being invaded by the French. Before he left, therefore, better relations had to be established with France, which was done in the Treaty of Noyon in August 1516. He was then free to leave for Spain.

In some ways Spain was very similar to the Netherlands. Both consisted of a collection of lands which were united by their ruler in name only, each retaining its different laws and institutions. In other ways they were different. The lack of festivities and ceremonial, such as Charles had known in the Netherlands, must have made Spain seem a less welcoming country than the one he had left. Spain's past history was very different to that of the Netherlands. In Spain there were recent memories of fighting the forces of Islam. For Castilians, in particular, their interest and concern had been in the Reconquest, of pushing forward the frontier of Christian Spain, as many of their fellow countrymen were now doing in the New World (America). They felt a great pride in their achievements and much dislike and distrust of foreigners, amongst whom they included people from other parts of Spain. It was in this country that Charles's brother, Ferdinand, had been born and brought up and many Spaniards would have preferred him to be king.

★ To the Spanish, their new king was a foreigner. A contemporary writer tells us that 'among Spaniards no foreigner is accounted of importance. They boast that they know for themselves, and that is enough'. What they most wanted was a king who would support Spanish interests and concerns; not those of other lands. Charles did not speak any Spanish language and had never visited Spain. His chief adviser was a Burgundian nobleman, the lord of Chièvres, Guillaume de Croy, and there were few Spaniards in his household. In addition, his early actions as king seemed designed to lead to resentment among the Spaniards rather than to reconcile them to his rule. Ximenez de Cisneros, the regent in Spain during the period between Ferdinand's death and Charles's arrival, was dismissed in spite of the way he had maintained control over Spain during Charles's absence. Favours and important Spanish offices were given away to Charles's Burgundian supporters. Chièvres himself gained an important post in the government of Castile; Adrian of Utrecht received the bishopric of Tortosa; but most anger was aroused by the granting of the main Archbishopric in Castile, that of Toledo, to Chièvres' nephew, Guillaume Jacques de Croy, who was only 16 years old. Further complaints were made about Spanish money being sent out of Spain to the Burgundian court. An additional cause for dissatisfaction was Charles's own election as Holy Roman Emperor on 28 June 1519. Most Spaniards saw this as a means of drawing Charles's attention away from his new kingdoms in Spain.

★ To be fully accepted, Charles had first to be acknowledged as king by the various Cortes of his new kingdoms. The Cortes of Castile held in Valladolid in 1518 started badly. Charles had been so ill-advised as to choose a Burgundian councillor, Jean le Sauvage, as president of the Cortes. The representatives of the towns immediately expressed their resentment and protested against the inclusion of a foreigner at a meeting of their Cortes. They requested further that Charles respect the laws and privileges of Castile, administer justice, remove foreigners from his service, and learn to speak Castilian. But the Cortes had little power to force acceptance of their will. Charles did, however, swear to respect the traditional laws of Castile as was customary, and in return was granted a subsidy of 600 000 ducats without conditions.

In Aragon, Charles had to receive the acceptance of each of the three

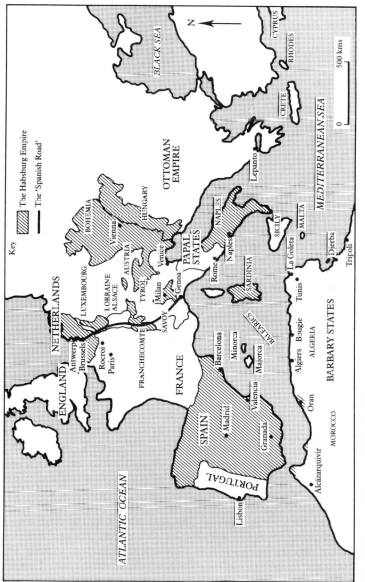

The Habsburg Empire of Charles V

separate Cortes. The Cortes of Aragon were more able to resist royal power than that of Castile and were even more reluctant to recognise Charles as king, particularly while his mother was still alive. It was not until January 1519 that they did so, and voted him a grant of 200 000 ducats. Acceptance by the Cortes of Catalonia, which met at Barcelona, took over a year to be agreed. Again there were objections to his Burgundian advisers, and it was only with reluctance that 250 000 ducats were granted to him. The delays therefore meant that Charles had no time to visit Valencia, the third main kingdom which made up the Crown of Aragon, for it was while at Barcelona that Charles received news, on 28th June 1519, that he had been elected Holy Roman Emperor.

* Charles needed to obtain money to pay the expenses incurred in becoming Holy Roman Emperor. He therefore called another Cortes in Castile in an attempt to acquire the necessary funds. It was at this Cortes that many of the concerns and fears of the Spanish were expressed. The Cortes was called to meet at Santiago in March 1520. This choice of meeting place created great annoyance. No Cortes had ever met in such a remote place before, and Santiago did not even have the right to send representatives to a Cortes. Further resentment was caused by the fact that the previous subsidy had been granted less than three years before. The representatives of many of the towns present tried to obtain discussion of their grievances before they would grant any money. Hardly surprisingly this did not suit Charles. Some of the representatives were bribed, and eventually a majority voted to approve the grant. Though Charles had made some concessions, the incident further increased the growing hostility to him. This was to find expression in the revolts which broke out later in the decade.

1 Rebellion

a) The *Comuneros*

The revolts of the 1520s in Spain mark a significant turning point in the reign, and their suppression was to help secure Charles's position. The more important was that which broke out in Castile in May 1520. Discontent had been growing for some months, not only in Castile, but elsewhere in the Spanish peninsula. There had already been a number of outbursts of violence, particularly in Aragon, before Charles left Spain for his coronation as Holy Roman Emperor in Germany. The major threat to his position, however, was the revolt which began in Castile on his departure. Though many areas of Castile were affected, most of the action took place in urban centres. The rebellion started in Toledo. Here, a member of the nobility, Juan de Padilla, took command and a government was set up in the name of the king, the queen (Joanna) and of the *communidad*, indicating that this was not a revolution aimed at overthrowing the king. Toledo's lead was followed by other towns such as Segovia, Salamanca and Valladolid, the residence of Charles's regent, the Burgundian, Adrian of Utrecht. Supporters of the rebellion came mostly from the lower nobility and town dwellers. All seem to have been resentful of Charles's leaving Spain, and to have hated the foreigners who filled important positions and offices. There were fears that their country would lose its separate identity as part of the Empire and that Charles would not return. Rumours even circulated that there would be taxes on the baptism of infants, on air and on water!

An attempt was made to gain the support of Queen Joanna when Tordesillas, where she was held prisoner, was taken. Although she was prepared to show her support when meeting with some of the *comuneros*, she would not commit herself to the rebellion on paper. This refusal left the leaders of the revolt with no claim to legality. Had they been able to say that they were attempting to restore the rightful monarch they would have had a clear purpose. As it was they had no clear aim in view.

The situation started to turn in favour of the king. Charles himself made some concessions. The collection of the subsidy voted by the Cortes of Santiago was stopped and two Castilians joined Adrian as regents. The character of the rebellion now changed. There were a few attacks on property and some demands were made for economic and social reforms, such as curbs on the powers of the nobles and the reduction of taxes. As a result more nobles were prepared to support the regents in trying to put down the revolt. A royal army was formed which defeated the *comuneros* at the Battle of Villalar in 1521. This was a major defeat. The *comuneros* lost control of most of northern Castile and only Toledo was able to hold out for a little longer.

Charles, on his return to Spain, was now in a position to deal firmly with those who had taken part in the revolt. The leaders were executed, but, apart from this, leniency was shown and a general pardon issued. The Crown increased its hold over the towns in Castile by increasing the powers of the *corregidores*, the royal officials who controlled town government. The eighteen towns previously represented in the Cortes were still able to send their representatives but there was little opposition to Crown policies and, though each king at the beginning of his reign still swore to uphold the liberties and privileges of Castile, this became only a formality.

This is not to support the view of some historians in the past who saw in the defeat of the *comuneros* the defeat of 'parliamentary' government and democracy in Castile and the victory of 'royal absolutism'. This would now be considered too extreme a view. No attempt was made to reduce the existing powers of the Cortes in either Castile or Aragon. Castile already had few means by which she could impinge on Charles's powers in the Cortes. The role of the nobility in government, particularly in local government, continued as before Villalar. Some historians argue that the nobility's authority and prestige were enhanced by their contribution to the victory over the *comuneros*. There were, however, complaints from some members of the nobility that they did not receive the rewards they felt entitled to after the victory. One wrote bitterly that Charles had 'not granted any *mercedes* [rewards] to those who took lance in hand with the result that Your Majesty is validating the proposition of those who say that the conflict was with the nobles and not with Your Majesty'. A more generally accepted view is that the failure of the *comuneros* meant a failure of purely Spanish interests. The defeat at Villalar signified the end of attempts to prevent Spain from playing a major role in the events of Europe – a role which Charles was determined to pursue and which was to have dramatic consequences for Spain's future.

b) The *Germania*

A second major revolt was also put down. This one had broken out in Valencia in 1519 and was much more of a social than a political revolt. The *Germania* was a Christian brotherhood of armed volunteers from the poorer classes which had been formed to defend the Valencian coast against Muslim pirates. Members of the *Germania* held grievances mainly against the local Muslims and the powers of the nobles who employed many of them. Plague had broken out in the area and this was seen by many as a punishment for tolerating the presence of Muslims in their community. There was also resentment against the privileges of the nobles and the near starvation conditions in which many members of the *Germania* lived. Further complaints were made against Charles who had frequently postponed the meeting of the Cortes of Valencia and did not seem interested in remaining in Spain. Support for the rebellion was therefore to be found among a wide section of the middle and lower classes – the poorer craftsmen, small farmers, weavers and spinners for example – but not among the nobles or wealthier clergy.

At first the violence of the movement was directed against the Muslim peasants in the country areas around Valencia: some were murdered and many were forcibly baptised into the Christian faith. As many of the rich had moved away from Valencia because of the plague, the supporters of the *Germania* were able to take over the city. They also experienced success against the small military forces sent against them which were led by nobles and representatives of the Crown. The movement spread beyond the city of Valencia to include most other parts of the kingdom of Aragon, even taking control of the island of Majorca. However, support was lost when a new leader, Vicent Peris, took over and incited his followers to more violence and to more radical demands, such as for a wider distribution of land. Many members of the middle classes, in particular, withdrew their support. As a result the supporters of the Crown made gains. The city of Valencia was recaptured, and an army of troops loyal to the nobles and to the Crown had defeated the undisciplined and ill-equipped army of the *Germania* by the end of 1521. Shortly after this defeat, Peris himself was captured and executed. Further resistance continued, but with much less support, until 1524 when the remaining areas in revolt surrendered. Many of the rebels were sentenced to death, others suffered fines and confiscations of their possessions. The local nobility had, by their victories, strengthened their own position.

c) Charles's Return to Spain, 1522

Charles's return to Spain in 1522 and the collapse of the revolts signalled a period of calm and growing acceptance of Charles by the Spanish. He was no longer a boy. He looked and acted more like a king and had gained in self-confidence. A description by an English statesman of the time calls him

> very wise and well understanding his affairs, right cold and temperate in speech with assured manner couching his words right well and to good purpose when he doth speak.

The lack of major events in the internal history of Spain after the two major revolts has often been remarked upon. It must, to some extent at least, be related to Charles's tactfulness and wisdom in his handling of the Spanish. It could also mean that he had learnt from previous mistakes. In a speech he made in 1529, he referred to the time when he left Spain in 1520 to become Holy Roman Emperor as a period when

> 1 I was managed and governed by M. de Chièvres, and I was not old enough to know these kingdoms or experienced enough to govern them. And as I left immediately for Flanders, having spent very little time here, and what is more, being still unmarried and
> 5 without an heir, it is not surprising that there was scandal and disturbance.

Perhaps lessons had also been learnt from the demands made during the *comuneros* revolt. Charles was certainly prepared to be more 'Spanish' on his return in 1522.

The language spoken by Charles and at his court was now Spanish, or rather Castilian. He made a popular marriage when, in 1526, he wedded his cousin Isabella, sister of the King of Portugal. There had been traditional links between Spain and Portugal, particularly during the reign of Isabella and Ferdinand, and Charles was to leave his wife to act as his regent during any absences he might have, knowing that, because of her Portuguese origins, her rule would probably be acceptable to his Spanish subjects. The following year, to great rejoicing, his first child and heir, Philip, was born in Castile. Spaniards, particularly Castilians, began to play a more important role in government. More and more Spaniards took offices in the administration, not only in Spain but also in other parts of the empire. The conquest of Mexico in 1521 by Cortés and that of Peru in 1525 by Pizarro led to the development of an empire in America which gave opportunities to many Castilians.

2 The Government of Spain

The Americas and Spain were only a part of Charles's personal empire. Reference to the map on page 35 gives some idea of the extent of the lands that Charles ruled. Opinions among historians differ as to how Charles saw his role in governing this empire. To some historians, his dream was of a universal monarchy. In 1519 Gattinara, the Italian who had become Charles's main adviser, wrote to him:

1   . . . now that God in His prodigious grace has elevated Your Majesty above all Kings and Princes of Christendom, to a pinnacle of power occupied before by none except your mighty predecessor Charlemagne, you are on the road towards Universal Monarchy
5   and on the point of uniting Christendom under a single shepherd.

It seemed possible to his contemporaries that Charles, with the amount of lands over which he ruled, could become the sole ruler over all Christian countries:

Christ has granted an extra-ordinary opportunity to the men of our age to realize this ideal, thanks to the great victory of the Emperor and the captivity of the Pope.

But there is little in Charles's own writings to support this view. In these it is to his House, his dynasty, that he continually refers, indicating that this was of major importance to him. In fact, when speaking to the Pope and cardinals in 1536, he denied that he had any idea of gathering a universal empire under his rule:

There are those who say that I wish to rule the world, but both my thoughts and my deeds demonstrate the contrary.

Charles did not seem to have any idea of even bringing all the lands over which he did rule under central control with common institutions. In any case, each of his lands would have resented any such attempt and he must have known this. It was concern for his dynasty and the need to protect his lands which led him into fighting wars almost continuously until his abdication. In addition, his commitment to Catholicism involved him in fighting wars to defend Catholicism against the growing Protestant threat within his own empire and against the Muslims from without. This involvement in so many areas of Europe meant that Charles was rarely in a position to concentrate on dealing with any one problem before he was called to deal with another. His Spanish subjects, though never completely reconciled to those responsibilities which took him out of Spain so much, did in general come to sympathise with him. It was Spanish, particularly Castilian, wealth and arms which supported him in many of his endeavours.

Charles remained in Spain after his return in 1522 until 1529. This was the longest time he spent in any one of his territories and he used the opportunity to try to establish his authority over the government of his kingdoms there. As with the other sections of his empire, Charles did not envisage joining the separate kingdoms of Spain into one or introducing a single institution through which he could govern the whole of Spain. Charles was King of Castile and King of Aragon, not King of Spain. On the other hand, if he was to have control over Spain, and in particular obtain the money he needed for his various enterprises, it was vital that he ensure his hold over the administration, especially that of the richest of his Spanish kingdoms, Castile.

a) The Councils

To this end Charles continued the reforms in conciliar government already begun by Ferdinand and Isabella. Councils were still the most important feature of the administrative system, composed not of the most important nobles but mainly of *letrados* (see page 17). At the same time, additions and changes needed to be made to the system for Charles to establish his control and for it to be able to meet the demands of running an empire as widespread as his.

The councils can be divided into two main types. The first was mainly advisory, and the second mainly administrative. The new Council of State set up in 1526 fell within the first category. In theory its purpose was to advise Charles on the most important matters concerning the government of Spain (and of Germany), and to deal with the decisions of the other councils. In practice its existence under Charles was probably designed to give social distinction to its members, who constantly attended the Emperor. It had little political influence and little administrative importance during Charles's reign.

A second advisory Council was that of War. This was also newly formed. It came into existence in 1522 and usually had the same membership as the Council of State, with the addition of military experts. Its responsibility was to co-ordinate all the military matters concerning the Crown.

The second main type of council was made up of those concerned with administration. Some of these dealt with the administration of geographical areas of Charles's empire, some with particular functions. The Royal Council of Castile was probably the most important of these – the one Charles referred to as 'the support of my realms'. It dealt with most of the internal affairs of Castile; acted as a court of law, hearing appeals from the lower courts, and advised the king on many matters, especially relations with Portugal, with which there were traditional links. Charles reduced the size of the council and included fewer nobles. Typical members were ecclesiastics and *letrados*, men who were thoroughly reliable but who tended to show little independence.

The Council of Aragon had already assumed many of the attributes of a modern bureaucracy under Ferdinand. Like the Council of Castile, it dealt mainly with the administration of justice, acting as the court of highest appeal, and had some internal administrative functions. Its officials were not from the nobility but were *letrados*. Charles generally respected the tradition that they should come from the three kingdoms of Aragon. An exception was the treasurer, who throughout Charles's lifetime was a Castilian. Another new Council was the Council of the Indies, formed in 1524 and given control over all matters concerning the running of Castile's American possessions.

There were also general administrative councils which were not linked specifically to geographical areas. One of the most important of these was the Council of Finance. This was originally created in 1522 for the management of Castile's finances, but it gradually assumed responsibility for all Charles's finances. The Council of the Supreme and General Inquisition was one of the few elements which linked all the kingdoms of Spain together, for it dealt with all matters of heresy not only in Castile but in all the kingdoms of Spain.

The new councils helped meet the increasing demands of administering an extended empire. However, they were in existence mainly to advise Charles. They were not responsible for making sure that decisions were implemented, and they had no officials with which to do this.

The effectiveness of government depended very much on Charles and his secretaries making the system work. The organisation of the secretariat was based in each kingdom, the most important one in Spain being in Castile. Aragon already had a highly organised secretariat – the Chancellery – which Charles retained. In Castile it was different. The secretaries here were responsible for preparing the agendas for council meetings; all royal documents had to be countersigned by them; when correspondence arrived it was they who decided whether it should go to Charles or to one of the councils. They could also issue royal decrees without the agreement of the council. Much patronage was at their command. Their powers therefore often caused resentment, particularly from the members of the councils themselves. However, because of the speed with which they were able to act, more use was made of them by Charles. Consequently, their powers increased during his reign. The most important secretary for much of Charles's reign was Francisco de los Cobos. His office dealt with the affairs of Castile, Portugal, the Indies and, from 1530, Italy. Cobos improved the quality of those working in the secretariat. He usually chose men from the minor gentry who had had administrative training and experience and came from the smaller towns. They were not the younger sons of nobles, nor necessarily men of learning or those with a university training. Those chosen by Cobos looked to him for their rewards and advancement. So he was able to rely on them to support him in his policies.

However, there were drawbacks as well as advantages to this. As the most important means of access to the king, Cobos received many gifts from those seeking to see or gain favours from Charles and, like other secretaries, he was able to acquire a large fortune and estate. Charles was prepared to accept this for he had no doubt of Cobos's personal loyalty and efficiency. These mattered more to Charles than concerns about the way in which Cobos had built up his fortune. Charles showed his opinion of Cobos in a letter to his son:

1 Cobos is growing older and easier to manage, but he is true. The danger with him is his ambitious wife. No one knows so much of all my affairs as he, and you will always have reason to be glad of his service. But do not give him more influence than I have sanctioned
5 in my instructions. And above all do not yield to any temptations he may throw in your path; . . . Cobos is a very rich man, for he draws a great deal from the dues for smelting bullion from the Indies, as also from the salt-mines and other sources. He looks on these things as his own particular privilege, but do not let them become
10 heritable in his family. When I die, perhaps, it would be a good moment to resume these rights to the Crown. He has great gifts in the management of finances; circumstances not he are to blame for the deplorable condition of our revenues.

To prevent excessive corruption it was important that Charles did not depend completely on his secretaries. He tried never to leave any matter entirely in the hands of his servants. He aimed to play some personal part in dealings on every issue. He sometimes wrote to his ministers and ambassadors himself, rather than relying on his secretaries to do so, and letters survive annotated in his own handwriting.

b) The Cortes

The Cortes of the individual Spanish kingdoms were a focus of possible resistance to Charles. But they could not make laws. They could only present petitions to the king who might or might not listen to them. The one important weapon they had was their ability to vote or to refuse money in the form of grants (a *servicio*) and to allow new taxes.

The three Cortes of Aragon had a long tradition of independence and of rights over taxation (see page 6). Charles called a General Cortes of the representatives of the three kingdoms to meet six times during his reign, but, though they met at the same place, Monzon, they each sat separately and had to be dealt with separately. In addition the individual Cortes met twice in Catalonia and once each in Aragon and Valencia. But it was hardly worthwhile Charles spending a long time persuading the representatives to grant him money, for even when they agreed a *servicio* it amounted to little and a third of it had to be spent on internal purposes. This meant that relatively little was available for the main reason for which Charles required it – the financing of his wars. It is therefore not surprising that the Cortes were not summoned very often.

More funds were obtainable, and more easily, from elsewhere, especially from Castile. The Castilian Cortes traditionally had fewer powers than those of Aragon and voted grants of money for Charles before discussing other matters. It usually consisted only of the representatives of the eighteen towns who had a right to meet there, not of the nobles or clergy. During Charles's reign, the Cortes met fifteen times, mainly to vote on the money that Charles so often desperately needed. An attempt was made, early in Charles's reign, at the 1523 meeting at Valladolid, to discuss general political matters before granting taxes but this was firmly dealt with by Charles:

1   Yesterday I asked you for funds; today I want your advice. Which seems to you better, that you should grant me the *servicio* at once, on my promise not to dismiss you until I have replied to and provided for everything that you justly ask me, and that I should do
5   so of my own free will; or that I should first reply to the petition which you bring me, and have it said that I do so in order to get the *servicio*? You know that the custom has been to grant this first; thus it was done under my royal predecessors. . . . Why try to establish an innovation with me? And since many evils have brought me to
10 this necessity, you, like good and loyal subjects, will remedy them by doing your duty as I expect you to do.

He was making it quite clear that taxes must be granted first, and that only then would the Cortes be free to discuss other matters.

Part of the reason for the lack of power of the Castilian Cortes was that only eighteen towns were able to send representatives (two each), and these did not represent all areas of the kingdom. In addition, the nobles and clergy were not usually called. However, in 1527, Charles was in desperate need of money for the campaign against the Turks in Eastern Europe and wanted the nobles and clergy to agree to a special grant. To this end he called a General Cortes. But both nobles and clergy feared that such a precedent would mean a loss of their right to freedom from taxation, so Charles obtained nothing except some private donations from members of the clergy. Nobles and clergy were also called to a Cortes at Toledo in 1538, when Charles was again in need of money. This time it was not only because of the campaigns fought in Germany, North Africa and France, and that proposed against the Turks, but also to help meet the ordinary expenses of government. Charles now asked for a new tax, on food, the *sisa*. Such a tax would clearly have to be paid by all in Castile, nobles and clergy as well as the rest of the population. Again the nobility refused. Charles realised that there was no point in continuing and dismissed this Cortes.

If Charles had failed to gain contributions from the richer elements in Castile, he was able to gain the agreement of the representatives of the towns to raise most of the money he requested. That they had little power to deny Charles is partly shown by the way the 1544 Cortes requested that they should not be summoned more frequently than once every three years 'on account of the great costs and expense'. They seem to be implying here that they knew they could do little more than agree to what Charles wanted.

Historians have debated whether or not there was a revolution in the development of government under Charles. Certainly administrative machinery had to evolve to meet the increasing demands of government. But, of course, the conciliar system itself already existed in Spain; Charles merely added to it and adapted it to meet his needs. The Councils of State and War were both new creations, but other councils were more clearly linked with what had gone before. With the expansion of lands under Charles's rule, the number of territorial councils consequently increased. These too looked back to previous reigns, being organised on the lines of the Council of Aragon already set up under Ferdinand. The administrative councils can all be traced back to earlier reigns. One major change, however, was that under Charles, secretaries such as Cobos grew in power and status.

Other instruments of government remained similar to those which had gone before. Members of Charles's family were appointed as governors or viceroys in important realms of the empire. There continued to be no fixed capital, though much administration was done in Valladolid. Like his grandparents, Isabella and Ferdinand, Charles was constantly on the move, accompanied by his secretaries and advisers. The powers of the Cortes in both Castile and the three kingdoms of Aragon remained unchanged. In local administration the Crown still had to rely on the nobles and others who were respected in the localities. The changes that did occur were important but in no real sense did they constitute a revolution.

c) Finance

Shortage of money was always Charles's main reason for calling a Cortes, and throughout his reign he had difficulties in meeting his financial needs. The Crown's financial position had not been strong when he became king. It worsened in the early years of his reign as a result of the greed of his Burgundian followers and the expenses of the imperial election. As early as 1523 he was saying that government debts in Castile 'amount to far more than I receive in revenue', at a time when all the prospective income for the following year had already been spent. His responsibilities as Emperor led to an enormous demand for money – fighting wars in the sixteenth century became very expensive. In addition to this there was the cost of the upkeep of his royal household. The cost of the ceremonial of the court had increased considerably compared to the cost under Isabella and Ferdinand, for Charles had made it more like the

Burgundian court to which he had been accustomed. Money had to be found to meet the salaries of the many new positions created, such as that of gentlemen of the household, and for the buying of jewels and works of art. All this amounted to about a tenth of the Crown's income.

Finance came from all parts of Charles's empire. Each area was expected to be self supporting and, in addition, to give support to the general needs of the Empire. The imperial coronation expenses were mainly paid for by Castile; at the end of his reign the Netherlands made the major contribution towards the wars against France; and payment for the armies to defend Vienna from the Turks in 1532 came from the Empire. Usually, however, there was reluctance for money raised to be used for anything other than the needs of the country from which it came. It was only money raised from Castile which was regularly used for the general expenses of the Empire.

It was Castile too, which contributed most of the income which came to Charles from Spain. There was little resistance from the Cortes to higher taxation. In any case the majority of taxes were indirect rather than personal and could be collected without the need to refer to the Cortes. The most significant of these was the *alcabala* – the sales tax – which all had to pay whatever their income. In 1534 it was argued that this should be a fixed sum and, because of continuing inflation, its value in real terms gradually fell. Of the other indirect taxes, only the customs duties made a valuable contribution. Charles did not manage to obtain any new taxes. However, he did establish the Crown's right to receive the *servicio*, granted by the Castilian Cortes, on a regular basis. This was the result partly of the defeat of the *comuneros* and partly because of the increase of royal power in the towns where the Crown was able to influence the selection of representatives to the Cortes. To obtain more of the country's wealth, Charles needed to able to tax more fully the richer social groups of his kingdom, particularly the nobility which paid little in taxes. The direct tax burden fell only on one section of Castile, the lower and middle classes. His failure to increase the taxation of the rich meant that he had to turn to borrowing. This was done partly through the sale of *juros*, bonds paying a set rate of interest, the interest payable being assigned to a specific source of ordinary revenue. However, as more and more loans were raised, less and less of the ordinary revenue, of course, came directly to the Crown.

Apart from Castile, the Spanish Crown had three sources of income. Firstly there was Aragon. But the constitution there meant that little could be raised in taxes. In any case, by Charles's reign, Aragon was not economically strong enough to be able to give him much financial help.

Secondly there was the Church. Although in theory it did not have to pay taxes, in practice it gave a great deal of money. The Pope allowed Charles to receive a proportion of all the income of the Spanish Church. In 1532, 372 000 ducats were raised in this way and by 1551 this had reached 500 000 ducats. A further source of income was the *cruzada*, a special contribution paid by both laity and clergy which, between 1523 and 1554, raised an average of 121 000 ducats a year. The money contributed in this way amounted to about a quarter of the royal income. The Crown had already gained control of the orders of military knighthood under Ferdinand and Isabella, and in 1523 the Pope declared that they were in the Crown's ownership for ever. However, partly as a result of the loans Charles received from the German banking house of the Fuggers for the cost of the Imperial election, the income from these military orders went there rather than to the Crown. As well as an annual income, the Church also provided gifts of money from time to time. Other sources of funds which went from the Church to the Crown included the income of sees between the death of one bishop and the appointment of his successor.

The third source of income was the wealth which went into Castile, particularly from the 1530s onwards, from America. This would seem to have been the solution to Spain's financial problems. Certainly the sums were high. Between 1534 and 1540, the average annual receipts were 324 000 ducats, between 1545 and 1550 – 382 000 ducats, and between 1551 and 1555 – 871 000 ducats. The Crown was entitled to revenue from taxes, customs duties, Indian tribute and, most significant, a fifth of all precious metals mined. There can be no doubt that income from America made a vital contribution to Charles's finances, but it did not provide the solution to all his financial problems. Even without any repayment of loans, one million ducats per year was needed for ordinary revenue. In addition to this were the expenses that Charles's foreign policy involved him in – the Metz campaign of 1552 alone cost over two million ducats.

Such, in fact, were Charles's problems over finance that in 1552 he started to resort to other measures to try to raise money, measures which were to make it even more difficult to manage the country's finances efficiently. Sales of public offices took place, which prevented the advancement of people according to their ability. There was also the sale of certificates of nobility, which further decreased the size of the tax-paying population and increased the burden falling on those who did still pay taxes.

The only way in which Charles could have improved his financial position was to cease fighting expensive wars. And this he felt unable to do.

d) Protestantism

The wars that Charles was fighting included those against Protestants in Europe. However, if he had little success in defending the Catholic faith against Protestantism in the Holy Roman Empire, matters were very different within the peninsula. Any signs of Protestantism were quickly eliminated. Two groups were considered to hold heretical views and became associated with Protestantism during the 1520s. One of these was the Illuminists and the other the Erasmists. Illuminism began among a group of friars and was a form of mysticism. The Illuminists believed that they could put themselves in direct, personal communication with God, and many, like the Protestants, believed that good works were useless. The Inquisition persecuted members of any group found and condemned their ideas as heretical. Of more importance were the Erasmists who were the followers of the Burgundian philosopher Erasmus. At first his ideas were well received in Spain and he gained many influential supporters, both at court and in the universities. Charles himself showed interest in his work. However, by the end of the 1520s Erasmianism had become associated with Protestantism and its adherents began to be persecuted by the Inquisition. Within ten years it had been almost totally wiped out in Spain. During the 1550s a few isolated cases of genuine Protestants were uncovered but these were easily repressed.

Steps were taken to try to prevent Protestant ideas entering the peninsula from abroad. Censorship was introduced and severe penalties were inflicted on anyone bringing books into Spain without a licence. This was followed by the Spanish Inquisition's own Index of Books by which certain works were subject wholly or in part to prohibition. Philip II continued the policies of his father when he returned to Spain as king after Charles's abdication in 1556 (see page 55). Spaniards were in future only allowed to study in Spain itself or at a few individual colleges abroad.

The effects of this policy have been greatly debated. Some historians take the view that this led to the complete isolation of Spain from the ideas of the rest of Europe. This did not happen completely, however, and it is doubtful if there was any major adverse effect on the development of Spain's culture during this period. It certainly does not seem to have prevented the flowering of original and creative literature and works of art during the following hundred years.

* How successful then was Charles's rule in Spain itself? In considering this one must always keep in mind that he was not just King of Spain. Spain was only one of the territories over which he ruled, and what happened in other parts of his empire frequently had implications for the policies he followed in Spain. As ruler of so many kingdoms and states in Europe, Charles was frequently brought into conflict with other powers, notably France. An additional burden for him was his position as Holy Roman Emperor. This brought him responsibilities as the principal defender of the Roman Catholic faith, both against the growing threat of Protestantism and against the powerful Turkish Empire. Conflict often meant war, which in turn made enormous demands on his finances.

One of Charles's main aims in ruling Spain was therefore to obtain the money necessary to fight the many wars in which he was involved. In addition, he was determined to establish himself securely as ruler of

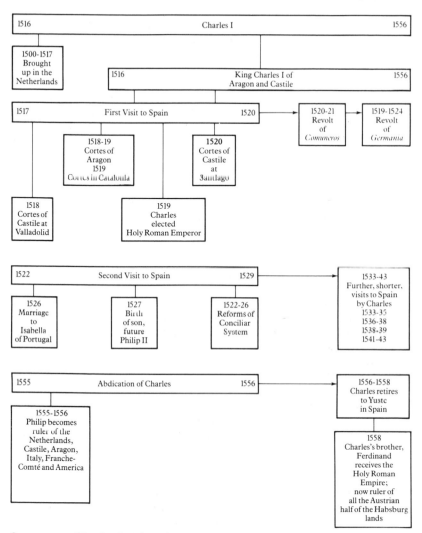

| 1516 | Charles I | 1556 |

| 1500-1517 Brought up in the Netherlands | | |
| 1516 | King Charles I of Aragon and Castile | 1556 |

| 1517 | First Visit to Spain | 1520 |
| 1520-21 Revolt of *Comuneros* | 1519-1524 Revolt of *Germania* |

| 1518-19 Cortes of Aragon 1519 Cortes in Cataluña | 1520 Cortes of Castile at Santiago |

| 1518 Cortes of Castile at Valladolid | 1519 Charles elected Holy Roman Emperor |

| 1522 | Second Visit to Spain | 1529 |
| 1533-43 Further, shorter, visits to Spain by Charles 1533-35 1536-38 1538-39 1541-43 |

| 1526 Marriage to Isabella of Portugal | 1527 Birth of son, future Philip II | 1522-26 Reforms of Conciliar System |

| 1555 | Abdication of Charles | 1556 |
| 1556-1558 Charles retires to Yuste in Spain |

| 1555-1556 Philip becomes ruler of the Netherlands, Castile, Aragon, Italy, Franche-Comté and America |

| 1558 Charles's brother, Ferdinand receives the Holy Roman Empire; now ruler of all the Austrian half of the Habsburg lands |

Summary – Charles I, 1516–56

Spain, and to safeguard the position of Roman Catholicism there. 'Exterminate heresy, lest it take root and overturn the state and the social order', were his orders to the regents he left to govern Spain during his many absences. For all three aims there was much with which Charles could be satisfied. After the *comuneros* and *germanías* revolts he encountered little opposition to his policies and no serious signs of discontent were apparent for the rest of his reign. Changes in the administration were made to improve the level of efficiency in the government of the Spanish kingdoms though the lack of means for putting decisions into effect must have hindered his attempts to be an effective ruler. Castile contributed much of the resources he needed to meet the growing demands of the empire. In addition, Charles's religious policies were far more successful in Spain than in the rest of the empire. In 1525 all Muslims in the Kingdom of Aragon had to become Christians or leave the country. The threat of Protestantism in Spain was swiftly and completely dealt with. In theory, at least, all the inhabitants of Spain were Roman Catholic, although suspicions remained that the converted Jews and Muslims were only nominal Christians.

Charles's subjects, though some grievances remained, had generally become reconciled to his rule. In Castile, in particular, the most influential nobles continued to play an important part in government and at the royal court – even though there were grumbles about the growing cost of the latter. In the non-Castilian kingdoms there was satisfaction that Charles was prepared to respect their particular laws and privileges, although there was some resentment at the number of positions and rewards which were reserved for Castilians. Those who must have felt most discontented were the Castilian tax-payers (especially those in the poorer agricultural areas), who were expected to pay ever increasing sums of money in taxes. But after the revolts of the 1520s, these were kept under control by the non-taxpaying nobles and clergy.

Whereas Charles was relatively satisfied with his achievements as king in Spain, historians looking back to this period with the advantage of hindsight and seeing more clearly the consequences of Charles's actions – or lack of them – have tended to be more critical. Major criticisms have been made in the area of finance. Although none of Charles's wars were fought in Spain itself, the kingdoms had to supply much of the money needed for the waging of these wars. The cost was so high that Charles's son had to declare a bankruptcy at the start of his reign in 1556. Charles's need for money also led to him obtaining loans from foreign bankers and using future Castilian revenues as security. This resulted in foreign bankers having an increasing hold over the royal income from Castile. Charles was mortgaging the future for the sake of the present. He felt that the defence of Roman Catholicism demanded this, but, in fact much of the money raised in loans was spent in furthering his dynastic rivalry with the King of France.

There has also been criticism of the steps that Charles took to ensure that Spain should not be open to foreign, often heretical, ideas. A list of prohibited books – the Spanish Index – had been first published in 1547. The government controlled which books were allowed into Spain, and licences were needed for the printing of any books and manuscripts. In one sense this could be counted a success, in that the Catholic faith was effectively protected, but a number of historians have seen the policy as damaging Spain's culture – her literature, the arts and science – by cutting her off from the culture of the rest of Europe. Other historians contend that this policy had little effect. In the final analysis, however, given the conditions and restraints in which Charles was acting and making decisions, one must say that, generally, his reign was one of success in Spain, if not in the rest of his empire.

Making notes on '*Charles I, 1516–1556*'

This chapter sets out the main features of the government of Charles I in Spain. You need to make outline notes on what he did – but not in great detail, as narrative is not usually required for this topic. Concentrate on his motives and, where relevant, the results of his actions. You should think carefully about the degree of Charles's success, i.e. in what ways was he successful and in what ways not?

The following headings and sub-headings should provide a framework for your notes:
1.   Problems on becoming king. (For each of the following sub-sections think particularly about 'In what ways did this create problems for Charles?')
1.1. Charles's Burgundian background
1.2. Attitude of Spanish to Charles
1.3. Charles acknowledged as king by the Cortes
1.4. Charles becomes Holy Roman Emperor
2.   Charles establishes his rule in Spain. (For each of the sub-sections think particularly about how Charles was able to secure his role in Spain.)
2.1. Defeat of *Comuneros* Revolt
2.2. Defeat of *Germania*
2.3. The Spanish become reconciled to his rule
3.   The Government of Spain. (For each of the sub-sections concentrate particularly on how much control Charles had, and how successful he was in achieving what he wished to do.)
3.1. Charles's attitude to governing his empire
3.2. The Councils
3.3. The Cortes
3.4. Charles's financial position
3.5. Dealing with Protestantism in Spain

Answering essay questions on Charles I, 1516–1556

You will meet few essay questions which deal only with Charles I and Spain. Usually the questions deal with Spain as part of the Empire and look for knowledge of such aspects as:
a) the problems Charles had to deal with in Spain
b) the methods Charles employed in ruling Spain

c) the degree of success Charles achieved
d) the problems Charles left to his son Philip II
  The type of question that is often found on Charles I and Spain is,

  'How successful was Charles I as king of Spain?'

If you have made notes as suggested, you should already have identified a number of topics as being relevant to this question. Make a list of these. You will probably have a list of about five points. Make sure that you have enough material to write one paragraph on each.

In writing this type of essay it is sometimes easiest to give the factual information first in each paragraph and to end *each* paragraph with your comments on the degree of success of Charles's policies. For each topic chosen there will probably be some ways in which Charles succeeded and some ways in which he failed. Comment on both. You should then write a few sentences at the very end giving an overall summary of Charles's success or otherwise. Bring in your own opinions here if at all possible.

However, a more effective essay is likely to result from adopting a more difficult approach. This involves writing a two-part essay. One part groups together all the aspects of his success; the other deals with his failures. A concluding paragraph explains whether successes outweighed failures, or *vice versa*. A-level candidates should be able to write this sort of essay by the end of their course.

Source-based questions on 'Charles I, 1516–1556'

1   Charles's character
Read the extracts on page 39 carefully and answer the following questions:
a) What do you learn about Charles's character from these two extracts?
b) What examples could be given to illustrate the validity of what Charles says of himself in 1520?
c) What changes had occurred in Charles by 1529? Suggest reasons why this might have happened.
d) What advantages and disadvantages are there for the historian using the two types of sources given here?

2   Charles's views on the Empire
Read the extracts on page 40 carefully and answer the following questions:
a) How do these extracts differ in what they have to say about governing the empire?
b) Comment on the tone and language used in each.

c) How realistic do you consider Gattinara's advice to Charles to be?
d) Using your own knowledge, how far do you consider that Charles is giving a truthful statement in the last extract?

3   Charles I on Cobos
Read the extract on page 43 carefully and answer the following questions:
a) What do you learn about Cobos's personality and abilities from this extract?
b) In what ways does Charles I advise Philip to be careful in his relationship with Cobos?
c) Do you think this is sensible advice for a king of the time to give? Give reasons for your answer.
d) What other types of evidence would you seek if you were a historian attempting to build up a fuller picture of Cobos?

CHAPTER 4

Philip II, 1556–98

1 Early Life and Character

Philip II, the only son of Charles I, was born in 1527. Unlike his father he was brought up and educated in Spain. From his birth his connection with Spain was therefore far closer than with any other part of the lands he was to rule. Although his tutors taught him subjects such as mathematics, Latin, Greek, architecture and history, no effort was made to teach him modern foreign languages. This was to prove a handicap for Philip who became fluent only in Castilian. He eventually came to understand Portuguese, French and Italian, but he was reluctant to speak them because of his poor pronounciation – a grave drawback for the ruler of a multi-lingual empire.

Like other princes he was taught the expected accomplishments of fencing, hunting and jousting, but, although he enjoyed riding, he seems to have derived most pleasure from dancing, playing the guitar and listening to music. He was an avid collector and reader of books, especially those of a religious nature. He also had an interest in nature study and a wide knowledge of birds, flowers and trees.

In character Philip seems to have taken after his mother, Isabella, rather than his father. In public he was reserved and dignified, conscious of his position, and showed emotional self control. Venetian ambassadors variously reported him as being:

1 white skinned and fair, very pleasantly built with a lip that hangs down a little. . . . He is very sluggish by nature but very dignified. He listens to people patiently . . . accompanies his answers with an amiable smile. He has a good memory and is extremely pious. . . .
5 He loves repose and solitude, particularly in summer. . . . He is never familiar with any of his servants, even with the most senior and intimate, but always preserves a gravity fitting to his royal dignity.

In his private life, however, he showed affection with close relatives and friends, as is evident in the letters he wrote to his two young daughters while he was in Portugal. He wonders in several of the letters if the girls are looking after their young brother, Diego:

1 I think he will have managed to fill in the coloured letters; this is why I am sending you others . . . and I've got some more. Make sure that he occupies himself in filling them in, but little by little, so as not to tire himself, and let him sometimes copy them. He will
5 learn more that way and I hope by this means acquire a good hand.

Philip shows anxiety over whether his youngest daughter Catalina would be scarred from the effects of smallpox:

Your sister and the Count write me to the effect that you won't have any marks, I mean scars, the others don't matter; they were only afraid there might be one near your nose . . . but if there are only a few, as I pray, then that's nothing.

Philip's political training was not neglected. Although his father was often out of Spain, and was therefore not personally present to counsel him, he sent a number of letters to Philip to guide him in his duties as a ruler. They contained advice that Philip was to try to follow throughout his life. Above all, his father wrote, he was to be:

1 a friend to justice. Command your servants that they be moved neither by passion nor by prejudice, still less by gifts. . . . In your bearing, be calm and reserved. Say nothing in anger. Be easy of approach and pleasant of manner. [Philip was to trust no-one fully]
5 Depend on no-one but yourself. Make sure of all but rely exclusively on none. In your perplexities trust always in your Maker. Have no care but for Him [God].

From the age of 12 Philip attended meetings of the royal councils. Early in 1543 he was appointed regent in Spain in Charles's absence and he held this position until 1548. It was then that he visited the other areas of the empire which were to become part of his inheritance, so that he might see and be seen by his future subjects. A short visit to Italy was followed by a longer one to the Netherlands. Charles's confidence in his son's abilities increased. His letters show him beginning to ask Philip's opinion on various political matters. In 1555, in a moving ceremony at Brussels, Charles, worn out by his responsibilities as Emperor, felt able to abdicate to Philip his rights in the Netherlands and Franche–Comté, Castile, Aragon and the Indies. It was now time for Philip, the prince 'who possesses many praiseworthy qualities', to take charge.

2 The Government of Spain

Philip's approach to the work of governing his kingdoms was very different to that of his father. He was far less outgoing than Charles. He preferred to stay in one place rather than to be on the move with his secretaries and advisers around him, which he did not believe to be an effective method of government. 'Travelling about one's kingdoms is neither useful nor decent', he wrote to his own son, the future Philip III. He established a permanent capital at Madrid, and rarely visited any of his territories outside of Spain. Also unlike his father, he preferred to communicate in writing with his officials, rather than in face to face conversation.

Philip was determined to know everything that was happening in his empire and to deal with all matters concerning its government himself. All important papers were meant to come to him to consider and sign. Often he would write comments on them in his spidery handwriting.

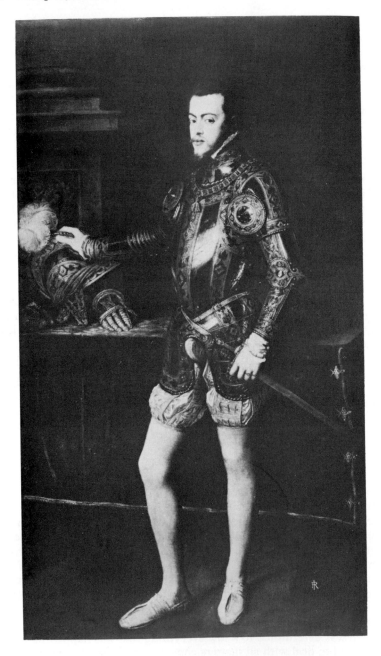

Portrait of Philip II by Titian. This was sent to England before his marriage to Mary I

Major problems were created by adopting such methods. The amount of written material was enormous and, despite his ability to remember factual material well, and his conscientious attitude to his work, he was unable to deal effectively with every matter that came to him. It is doubtful if any human being could. There is on record an account of one day in his reign when he read and signed four hundred separate documents. Even this rate of work was not enough, and sometimes, through tiredness of eyestrain or sheer exhaustion, he had to give up. One can visualise him fighting to keep awake as he wrote:

1   I have just been given this other packet of papers from you. I have neither the time nor the strength to look at it, and so I will not open it until tomorrow. It is already past ten o'clock and I have not yet dined. My table is full of papers for tomorrow because I cannot
5   cope with any more now.

Working in this way meant that Philip was, in theory, the only person with complete knowledge about a matter on which a decision had to be made. No-one had as much information as he did. His advisers and officials would only know about some aspects of any matter. This meant that they could only give advice based on their limited knowledge. Lack of time and energy to investigate a matter fully meant bad decisions might be made by Philip. It was a problem of which those who worked closest to him were well aware:

1   His Majesty makes mistakes and will continue to make mistakes in many matters because he discusses them with different people, sometimes with one, at other times with another, concealing something from one minister and revealing it to another. It is
5   therefore small wonder that different and even contradictory decisions are issued.

Philip's wish to deal with all important matters himself also meant that there could be long delays in communicating with the more distant parts of the Empire. It took at least two weeks for messages to travel from Madrid to Brussels in the Netherlands or to Milan in Italy, and at least another two weeks for a reply to be received. Two months was a short time for a letter to reach Mexico. By the time messages had been sent and replies had been received, the circumstances over which Philip had made a decision might well have changed and new orders might well be needed. However, once one action had been set in motion it was very difficult, if not impossible, to alter it in response to new circumstances. The problem of communication in such a vast empire as Philip possessed was the source of many difficulties.

If there were so many drawbacks to this system of working, why did Philip use it? The most obvious answer is that Philip was highly conscientious, wanting to do what was best for the people he governed. He thought that he could only do this by giving personal attention to every issue. A further explanation might be that Philip wished to ponder his decision at length because he was reluctant to trust anyone fully. His father's advice and his own experience made him hesitate to have complete faith in anyone. Philip showed on the death of one of his councillors that he felt he had allowed him too much power, 'I believed that it was wise to entrust many matters which concerned my royal office to . . . And perhaps there were good reasons for it then. But experience has shown that it was not a good thing; and although it meant more leisure and less work for me, I do not think it should be allowed to continue'. The need to consider an issue for the amount of time Philip often spent on it has been seen by others, then and now, as indicating an inability to make decisions. Certainly Philip's appointment of Requesens as governor of the Netherlands shows him unable to make up his mind. For ten months after his appointment, Requesens did not know whether he was a permanent or a temporary governor, or what he was expected to do there. However, Philip could act decisively on occasions, as he did during the events leading up to his becoming King of Portugal (see pages 67–9).

* Philip, as king, was forced to rely heavily on the advice he was given. He therefore tried to improve both the quality and quantity of the information upon which he based his decisions. Government became more centralised in some ways. In 1561 all central government offices were located in Madrid. A special depository was set up for government papers so that these could be called upon more easily when required.

The conciliar system remained, but with modifications. The Council of State, officially the main council, continued to be a forum in which important Castilian nobles could offer advice to the king, although it seems to have had little power. A Venetian wrote in 1557:

1 At the court the opinion about this Council is that it is not the source of such advice, deliberations, and performances as make for the honour and advantage of the king . . . for there seem to be no written rules or customs to produce order in its deliberations or
5 decisions, nor is membership in it either convenient or dignified; and the result is a decline in the vitality of its discussions.

The regional councils were more important. They were reorganised to try to make them more effective. Each was to meet regularly at fixed times on fixed days. Five new councils were created, including a Council of Italy and a Council of Portugal.

As Philip rarely attended meetings of the councils himself, he made great use of his secretaries. These were of vital importance. They served as intermediaries between Philip and the councils, taking the *consultas* (the reports summarising what had happened at each meeting of the councils) to the king and relaying his views to the council. The routine business was dealt with by ordinary royal secretaries, one of which was attached to each of the regional councils. But all important papers and requests that arrived at court were dealt with personally by Philip and his principal secretary.

As the king grew older it took much longer for him to deal with the ever increasing business. The structure of government was therefore changed in some respects after 1580. A system of *juntas* (informal committees) was set up. They were expected to discuss and advise the king on particular problems. They were not permanent bodies. Some might last for a few weeks, others for longer. Those who sat on the juntas were ministers and officials thought to be well informed about the problem being dealt with. Even within the juntas themselves there was an inner group, consisting of the king, three of his closest advisers, on whose word he felt he could rely, and his private secretary, who, for many years, was the hardworking, loyal and indispensable Mateo Vázquez. This group was referred to as the Junta of the Night because of the time at which it usually met, to discuss the business of the day and probably to decide on policy. Vázquez was a key figure in making this system work. As well as his position on the Junta of the Night he also acted as the co-ordinator of all the work of the juntas.

* Money problems were to pursue Philip as they had done his father. Left a large debt by Charles, Philip had no option but to suspend payments on all his debts in January 1557. However, he was not in a position to cancel his debts completely. Had he done this, few bankers would have agreed to lend him money in the future. What he did was to come to an agreement with his creditors that he would pay off his old debts at a lower rate of interest, while continuing to receive fresh loans. It meant that the foreign bankers lending him money, especially those from Germany and Genoa, would be prepared to continue to deliver the money to whichever part of Philip's empire they were asked. Without this facility Philip would have had considerable difficulties in paying his armies.

A poor financial start was not helped by the fact that Philip's territories, like most others in Europe at the time, were suffering from inflation. He therefore had to find increasing amounts of money to pay both for the ordinary expenses of government and for the cost of wars, which made major demands on his income.

To meet his financial needs, Philip could have either reduced his expenditure, increased his income, or borrowed. He tried all three. He made efforts to bring down the expenses of his household, in which he met with some success. However, the cost of the household was little in comparison to the cost of fighting wars. Military and naval requirements were becoming increasingly expensive. Not only had payments to be made to the fighting forces but money had also to be found for a wide range of materials and equipment, especially for the navy. It was only in these areas that significant savings might have been made, but Philip was not prepared to do this.

Philip had more success in increasing his income, at least in Castile and the Americas. Each part of the Empire was supposed to raise enough money for its own needs. In addition the king could in theory ask for money to meet the more general needs which concerned the whole of the Empire. But most of his territories had difficulty in raising money even for their own requirements. The Netherlands, which had provided his father Charles with a great deal of income, were not able to do so under Philip. In fact the reverse was true. Once part of the Netherlands had revolted against his rule, more and more of his resources were needed to try to deal with the uprising there. It was only from Castile and the Americas that he could depend on obtaining more.

In Castile there was little that the inhabitants could do to prevent Philip raising as much money as he wished. He was able to obtain subsidies from the Cortes at regular intervals and with little difficulty. The *alcabala* (the sales tax) was increased during his reign. The rate at which it was levied was first doubled and later tripled.

After the failure of the Armada in 1588 against England, the Castilian Cortes agreed to a tax called the *millones* (a duty on articles such as wine, oil and vinegar, which were bought regularly by everyone). This would have to be paid by all, whatever their income. Hardly surprisingly, the fact that it had to be paid on everyday articles meant it became the most unpopular of all the taxes in Castile.

The receipts from customs duties were increased. New duties were imposed and the rates on salt, an essential item, were raised. Philip also regained control of the customs houses, which meant that the Crown received customs duties directly, instead of via tax farmers who retained a significant proportion of what they collected.

The church also increased its contribution. The most important revenue from this source was the *cruzada*. The *cruzada* was a money offering paid for the fight against the Turks. In return the giver received spiritual benefits, including the forgiveness of sins. The *cruzada* continued to be paid regularly, and the amount collected doubled during the reign of Philip. The existing *subsidio* (a tax on rents, lands and other forms of income) and royal tithes also increased their yield. In addition a new tax was granted by the Pope in 1567. This was the *excusado*, a tax on the property of each parish.

Philip was particularly fortunate over the Indies, from which his annual income increased fourfold between 1560 and 1600. By the end of the century revenues from the Indies made up about 20 per cent of the Crown's total income. This was not as much as some contemporaries seem to have imagined it to be. Philip received a similar amount from the various clerical sources and more from taxes levied in Castile. But it helped considerably in giving an extra boost to his income to help pay for the wars in which Spain was involved.

Philip also tried to ensure that he received all of the income which was due to him. The financial departments of the government were reformed to try to make them more efficient. Attempts were made to prevent those in public office gaining an excessive amount of financial reward. At a time when such offices were low paid a certain amount of corruption and bribery was acceptable. No one, however, was allowed to receive excessive amounts in this way.

Yet there was never enough income for Philip to meet his expenses. He attempted, never with complete success, to bridge the gap by borrowing. As a result, he left long-term debts of about 68 million ducats to his successors – nearly three times the size of the debt he had inherited himself.

3 The Empire

Philip had not inherited all the territory that his father had held. The title of Holy Roman Emperor and the Habsburg family lands had gone to Ferdinand, brother of Charles, and his family. But, during his reign, Philip's own lands were to increase, particularly overseas, to create a new empire based on Spain. Not only did the Spanish overseas empire grow considerably in size but, with the inheritance of Portugal, he also acquired the vast Portuguese empire.

Philip viewed his empire from the perspective of Madrid. He did not have firsthand evidence of what was taking place. He had to rely on what he was told, whether by inhabitants of the various regions visiting Madrid, or by reports, given him by his own advisers or representatives in the different territories. This often meant that he received only one view of what was happening in any part of his empire, a view which was frequently inaccurate and out of date by the time he received it.

It is often difficult for us to understand, as we look back to the sixteenth century from our twentieth century standpoint, just how much religion and religious belief mattered. They cannot be distinguished from political considerations. Few rulers even contemplated allowing more than one religion to be practised in their lands. Philip was therefore not unusual in his determination that in the empire he ruled there should only be one religion – Roman Catholicism:

> Before suffering the slightest damage to religion and the service of
> God, I would lose all my estates, and a hundred lives if I had them
> because I do not wish, nor do I desire, to be the ruler of heretics.

Roman Catholicism needed to be defended not only against Protestantism but also against the threat of Islam. Defence against both were as fundamental to Philip's policies as they had been to his father's.

Apart from the defence of religion, Philip's other main aim in ruling his empire was to retain control of all his territories. He was determined to safeguard the interests of his family, his dynasty, and to hand his inheritance on to his successor undiminished.

The Netherlands were particularly vulnerable. They were near to the strongholds of Protestant power in England (from 1558) and the

Lutheran states in Germany. To the south and separating them from Spain lay France, by now a traditional enemy of Spain.

To protect the Netherlands, Philip had to defend the routes which linked them with Spain both by sea and by land (see map page 35). The sea route was frequently difficult, even in peacetime, due both to weather conditions and to piracy. The land route, 'the Spanish Road' which started from Genoa, had therefore to be kept open at all times. This meant that Philip had to ensure good relations with those rulers through whose territory the route passed. Need for finance also meant that particular care had to be taken to ensure that the treasure fleets from America were able to make their journeys across the Atlantic safely. A third major area of vulnerability was the Mediterranean, where there was intense rivalry with the Turks. The preservation of his sea routes in the Mediterranean and of his possessions there, particularly in Italy, was Philip's major concern at the beginning of his reign.

It is sometimes forgotten that even within the Iberian Peninsula itself there was considerable concern about security. There were fears for Roman Catholicism and concern for the 'purity of the faith'. A constant watch was kept on *moriscos* and *conversos* to prevent them reverting to any aspect of their former faith, and to ensure that Protestantism did not enter the peninsula. Nor was the country itself considered safe from military attack. In 1590, the secretary of war was concerned about the

1   miserable state of the monarchy, for which the only remedy and
    hope is to fortify Gibraltar, Perpignan, Navarre and the other fron-
    tiers . . . and to surround Madrid with fortresses, praying to God
    to give us the time, and in his mercy not punish us for our
5   sins. . . .

a) The Indies

Further increases to the territories over which Philip ruled took place outside Europe. In South America the Spanish conquistadors advanced south from Paraguay and established Buenos Aires in 1580. In Asia the Philippines, named after Philip, were taken over with little opposition in 1565. Added to this was the acquisition of the whole of Portugal's overseas empire in 1580 (see pages 67–9).

Philip depended on receiving the riches which came from the Indies, principally in the form of silver, but also as customs duties and the income from certain crown monopolies such as the sale of playing cards. Later in his reign, the *alcabala* was introduced in both Mexico and Peru. It was obviously important that the silver arrived safely in Europe, although this was made difficult by attacks on the treasure ships. As early as the mid-1520s French privateers had seized part of a treasure fleet. A number of Spanish towns in the Indies had been raided and plundered; shipping had been destroyed and further treasure had been taken. There had even been attempts to establish a French colony in Florida, but this had failed. From the mid-1550s the English became active in the area. Francis Drake made a number of daring raids on towns and shipping in the Caribbean and along the coast of Peru.

During Philip's reign a convoy system was introduced to protect the twice yearly treasure fleets as they made voyages across the Atlantic. Other ships patrolled in the seas near the Spanish coasts to protect the treasure as it arrived in Spanish waters. The scheme was expensive but it worked. No complete treasure fleet was ever captured in the sixteenth century. The only losses were a few scattered ships which had become separated from the main convoy.

Philip was also concerned to see effective administration and justice in the Indies. The problems involved were formidable. Not least of these was the distance between the Indies and Spain. There was also the difficulty of ruling a population which was largely unfamiliar with European ways. Yet much was accomplished. The Council of the Indies was responsible for a number of changes aimed at improving the effectiveness of the government. Viceroys were carefully selected from men of ability. An outstanding choice was Toledo, appointed viceroy to Peru in 1569, who brought peace and prosperity to this area. Attention was paid to the condition of the Indians. The 'New Laws for the Government of the Indies and good treatment and preservation of the Indians' were issued, which, among other things, forbade the enslavement of Indians. The intentions on the Crown's part were sincere, but the laws met such opposition from the Spanish settlers that it was impossible to implement them fully. A general Indies Court was set up to which individual Indians could bring complaints of abuse but few dared to do so. The religious life of the Indies was not neglected. Missionaries had always sailed with the fleets going from Spain to the Indies, but their impact had been limited. It was not until after 1580 that large scale attempts were made to convert the Indians.

b) Aragon

For the first part of his reign Philip paid little attention to Aragon. He rarely visited it and held few Cortes there. Nor did he press it to vote him more money than it could easily pay. Some of the reasons for this are contained in a report made by the Venetian ambassador in 1581:

1 The people of Aragon claim to be independent, as in effect they are, since they govern themselves almost as if Aragon were a republic. The king is the head of the state, but he does not inherit the position, they elect him to it. He appoints no official there except a
5 viceroy, who has no part in governing the land or administering justice. These tasks are the responsibilities of officials elected in that kingdom. The viceroy has charge only of the armed forces, and

the safety and defence of the region. His Majesty collects no revenue
from this region unless he goes there to conduct a meeting
10 of the Cortes, in which case they grant him 600 000 ducats. They
keep the rest of the taxes and duties and spend them for the benefit
of their own land. They guard their liberties very jealously and
bitterly contest each point so that the king and his ministers cannot
enlarge their control over them. As a result they frequently and
15 unnecessarily hinder measures which are not their business.

Philip probably felt, as his father had done, that the Aragonese had
neither the men nor the money to assist him more than they did.

By the 1580s, however, Philip decided that he had to intervene more
positively in the affairs of the kingdoms of Aragon. There were several
reasons for this. He had failed in an attempt to buy the county of
Ribagorza, on the border with France, from the noble who held it. He
needed Ribagorza to improve security on the frontier with France. In
addition, many Huguenots (French Protestants) had settled just across
the frontier in France. Philip feared that heresy would spread from
France into Spain. He also seems to have felt that he was failing in his
duty as king to secure justice for his people in Aragon. Banditry and
lawlessness in all three kingdoms, as well as pirate raids along the coast,
were reaching unacceptable levels.

At first troops were sent into Valencia to defend the coast against a
possible landing by North African pirates. Many complained that this
was clearly against the privileges of the kingdom, as the entry of foreign
soldiers was not allowed. Then a viceroy was sent to the kingdom of
Aragon who was not a native of the country. This again aroused an outcry
as it was claimed that all royal officials in the country should be Aragonese. Philip took the case to the *justicia* on the grounds that this
privilege did not apply to the office of viceroy. He argued that both
Charles and Ferdinand had in the past appointed Castilians to this post.
The *justicia* found in his favour. Soldiers from Aragon were sent in to
occupy Ribagorza claiming that law and order had broken down in the
area, and in 1591 the county became a possession of the Crown.

To complicate matters, a minor rebellion broke out in Aragon in 1591.
Antonio Pérez, Philip's disgraced former chief secretary, had escaped to
Aragon from his place of imprisonment in Castile. Pérez claimed his
right as a citizen of Aragon to be tried in the court of the *justicia*. Philip
tried to arrange for the case to be transferred to the court of the Inquisition. This was seen by many as an infringement of the rights of the
Aragonese. Others, particularly the lesser nobility, suspected that this
was Philip's first step in taking away their local power. Still others felt
resentful that they could not obtain offices or financial rewards from the
king for themselves or their sons. Many grumbled that these rewards
went to the Castilians alone. The Aragonese, or at least some of them, felt
they would be better off if they were independent. But few joined in the

rebellion which broke out and which was mainly confined to the town of Saragossa. Philip decided to send in an army to crush the revolt, even though this was against the privileges of Aragon. The army dealt with the rebellion swiftly. The leading rebels were executed, but Pérez himself fled to France.

Philip's army was in Aragon. He was now in a position to impose a settlement on the kingdom which would have subjected it more closely to his authority. He could have reduced the powers of the *justicia* and of the Cortes to enable him to control the kingdom in the same way that he controlled Castile. But he did not. Three reasons have been suggested by historians for this decision. As no one in Catalonia or Valencia had played a part in the revolt, and as even in Aragon the majority of the people had distanced themselves from it, it may not have seemed 'just' to Philip to punish the majority for the faults of the few. It may even have been that Philip did not have any intention of altering the traditional government of his kingdom. Or perhaps he may not have felt that the gains from such a move were worthwhile. The kingdom of Aragon was not particularly rich and Philip may not have felt that there was any point in spending time imposing his power to acquire so little.

Philip declared that his 'intention is only to keep their Charter and not allow people to contravene it'. He generally kept to the traditional forms of government in Aragon, although he introduced a number of changes which increased his power there. At the Cortes of 1592 he was given the right to dismiss the *justicia* when he wished. It was also clearly established that he was entitled to appoint a 'foreigner' as viceroy if he wished. It was agreed that measures presented at the Cortes would become law if a majority of those present voted for them, rather than there being a need for unanimous agreement. The permanent committee of the Cortes lost much of the control it had had over deciding on the use of the revenues of Aragon. Apart from these measures the constitution of the kingdom of Aragon remained unchanged. The measures taken were moderate and generally necessary to ensure good government in Aragon. There is no evidence here of Philip acting as a tyrant as he has been accused of doing by some historians.

c) The *Moriscos*

Another internal threat that Philip had to deal with was the revolt of the *moriscos* in Granada. There had officially been no members of the Muslim faith in Spain since 1526 (see pages 21–2 and 50). Those who had been Muslims were now Christians, known as 'new' Christians or *moriscos*.

People forced into conversion are hardly likely to be sincere believers. Philip continued the policy of attempting to make *moriscos* genuine converts through the teaching and the example of missionaries. This was a difficult task. Much depended on the quality of the clergy involved in the missionary work, and this varied greatly. Some of the clergy put a great deal of effort into their task. Most seem to have done little. As long as the *moriscos* attended mass and performed the outward signs of the Christian religion, little more was expected of them. It is not surprising, therefore, that most *moriscos* retained at least some of the practices of their old faith. Arabic was still spoken by some. Circumcision was common. They usually married within their own community, and generally followed their traditional way of life with its different diet and dress. Regular visits were made to the public baths around which their social lives centred.

By the late 1560s Philip decided that the policy of ensuring that the *moriscos* gradually became genuine Christians would have to be changed. Many of the Christian clergy had long been demanding that something more be done to deal with a group who seemed to be Christian in name alone. This demand cannot have failed to influence Philip, who was so committed to the Catholic faith. But of more concern to many in Spain, particularly the military commanders, was the security threat posed by the *moriscos*. The *moriscos* have been aptly described as a possible 'enemy within' prepared to help the Turks in their thrust across the western Mediterranean or the Muslim pirates, particularly from North Africa, who attacked villages and shipping along the coasts of Spain. There were also fears that the *moriscos* might join with the Protestants in southern France in any attack on Spanish soil. At a time when Philip was feeling that Christianity was on the defensive against the Muslim threat in the western Mediterranean, he was particularly concerned about any possible help that the Turks might receive from his own subjects. Although such fears were greatly exaggerated, there is certainly evidence of correspondence between *moriscos* and Muslims in both North Africa and the Turkish Empire. It appears to have been mainly for these reasons of security that the decision was made to take sterner measures against the *moriscos* in Granada.

The new policy began in 1567. *Moriscos* were forbidden to use Arabic, to wear their distinctive dress, to read Moorish literature, or to follow any other of their traditional customs. In many cases the new regulations were enforced harshly. In addition, many *moriscos* were already suffering economic hardships as a result of a depression in the silk industry where many earned their living.

Driven to despair, large numbers of *moriscos* joined a revolt which broke out near Granada in 1568. The government was unprepared. Its best troops were fighting in the Netherlands. There was no clear plan of how to deal with the revolt, which was to continue for two years. The fighting was marked by cruelty and massacres on both sides, until the *moriscos* were eventually defeated by government forces in 1570.

The *moriscos* were dealt with severely. An attempt was made to ensure that they did not live together as a group, but were spread throughout the Christian population. In this way, it was hoped, they would not present such a security threat and would be more likely to conform to a Christian way of life. All those not killed or made slaves were expelled from Granada and sent to other areas of Spain. Granada's population fell by more than a quarter between 1561 and 1591.

This method of dealing with the *moriscos* was not a success. Many *moriscos* were now in areas of Spain in which they had rarely been seen before. The fears, suspicions and jealousies of many more 'old' Christians than before were now aroused and resentment against them became more widespread. The dispersal had not dealt with the security threat that the *moriscos* presented. Plots and conspiracies involving Turks and French Protestants are revealed in surviving letters, sent or received by *moriscos*. A number turned to banditry or piracy.

Some of Philip's advisers urged him to expel the *moriscos* completely from the country. But Philip did not accept this advice. He was aware that there would be great opposition to such a move from those in Valencia who had many *moriscos* working on their estates. Instead, the number of missionaries working among the *moriscos* was increased. However, this had as little effect as before. The policy of assimilation had failed.

d) Portugal

One of Philip's major aspirations was to unify the Iberian Peninsula. The opportunity for achieving this came in 1578 when his nephew, Sebastian, King of Portugal, died fighting the Moors at the Battle of Alcazarquivir in Morocco. Sebastian's heir was his great uncle Cardinal Henry, aged 66, ill in health and vowed to celibacy. It was unlikely that Henry would live for much longer, and it was not clear who would succeed him.

There were several claimants to the throne but Philip's claim, through his mother Isabella, was one of the strongest and one which he was determined to pursue. By adding Portugal to his empire, Philip would unite under his rule all the kingdoms of the Iberian Peninsula. In addition he would acquire an overseas empire to match his own. For one of the few occasions in his life Philip acted decisively. One of his councillors, a Portuguese, was sent with money to arrange any necessary bribes and to persuade the nobility in Portugal of the rightness of Philip's case. An army was made ready under the Duke of Alba, Philip's most experienced general, in case an invasion of Portugal proved necessary.

Philip had support in Portugal for his claim. Both the nobles and the clergy, particularly the religious order of the Jesuits, were favourable. Philip had gained the support of many of the nobles by his payment of their ransoms after the Battle of Alcazarquivir. Merchants hoping to gain a share in trade with the Americas were also in favour. The writer of a letter from Lisbon, capital of Portugal, to one of the banking houses in Germany declared in 1580:

1   . . . all the best people here are in favour of Spain, but dare not let it
     be seen. . . . When the King of Spain appears here with his army he
     will be better received than he expects. . . . I fancy the authorities
     set up in this country have an understanding with the Spaniards. I
5   have no doubt that Spain will take possession of Portugal, as is
     fitting. I hope that then there will be better government and better
     business.

Opposed to him were the towns and most of the ordinary Portuguese.
Their hatred of the Spanish led them mainly to support another claimant
to the throne, Antonio, Prior of Crato, an illegitimate son of a brother of
Cardinal Henry.

No decision as to his successor had been made when Henry died in
1580. Both Antonio and Philip decided to pursue their claims. Philip
invaded Portugal before opposition could be organised. His forces
quickly captured Lisbon and defeated Antonio's army. Antonio was
forced to flee to France while Philip added Portugal to his empire.

Philip showed considerable skill in his dealings with the Portuguese in
order to make himself acceptable as their new ruler. His entry to Lisbon
shows the care he took over this. He wrote to his daughters that 'You will
have heard that they want to dress me in brocade, much against my will,
but they tell me it's the custom here'. He was prepared not only to wear
Portuguese dress but also cut his beard in the Portuguese fashion. He
tried to learn the language and even thought about moving his capital to
Lisbon, where he lived happily between December 1580 and February
1583. Philip tried to make it clear that Portugal was not going to become a
part of Spain but would be able to keep her own distinctive customs and
laws. When he was recognised as king by the Portuguese Cortes in 1581
he swore to respect the laws of Portugal. He agreed to a number of
measures which would enable Portugal to remain independent of Castile
in every way. Only Portuguese were to hold office in their kingdoms and
overseas possessions. The Cortes would not be required to meet outside
Portugal. The country would retain its own coinage. A Council of
Portugal was to be formed, like the other regional councils, to advise
Philip on Portuguese affairs. Philip's representative in Portugal, the
viceroy, was to be either Portuguese or a member of the Spanish royal
family.

Philip's rule was generally accepted by the Portuguese. His first choice
of representative was a wise one. The Archduke Albert of Austria, his
favourite nephew, was a well respected young man of 23. Under him
Portugal prospered and was well governed. However, not everybody
accepted Spanish rule. There were still many ordinary Portuguese who
refused to accept that Sebastian was dead and who thought that he might
some day return to drive out the Spanish intruder.

Philip's addition of Portugal to his empire has been considered to be
probably the most successful exploit of his reign. For the first time since

the Roman period the Iberian peninsula was under one Christian ruler. Philip had acquired another vast overseas empire. Possession of the Portuguese Azores gave the Spanish an important base for fleets sailing to Spain from the Indies. Portugal was important strategically. It was now unlikely that the country could be used as a base for foreign intervention which had been a Spanish fear when she had been a separate kingdom. The acquisition of Portuguese ports gave Philip a greater opportunity to involve himself in the affairs of Northern Europe and, if necessary, to launch an attack on England. No wonder that England in particular should fear this great increase in Spain's power.

e) The Mediterranean

Philip, as the chief defender of the Catholic faith, could consider no cause more righteous than that against the Turks and other Muslims. To the peoples of Spain with their tradition of the Reconquest, the Turks and all Muslims were their natural enemies. However, Philip was rarely in a position to concentrate all his efforts on dealing with the Muslims. Problems in other areas of his vast empire, and a lack of money prevented this. His aim was therefore mainly defensive; to fortify coasts, and to do whatever he could to help maintain the safety of those areas he ruled in the western and central areas of the Mediterranean.

There were three major concerns for Philip. The Turkish navy was in control of the eastern Mediterranean and posed a threat to its central and western areas. In nearly every year of Philip's reign fears were raised in all Christian areas along the coasts of the Mediterranean that a large Turkish fleet was on the offensive. Along the coast of northern Africa were bases such as Tunis and Algiers from which the Barbary corsairs (pirates) were able to attack shipping and raid the coasts of Spain itself. Within Spain, as we have seen above, were the *moriscos*, who might have co-operated with any Muslim invasion of Spain.

In 1560 an expedition was mounted against Tripoli to help protect the central Mediterranean area. All that was accomplished, however, was the capture of one island, Djerba, which was soon lost again. Spanish failure here was a blow to its prestige. It also led Philip to revise his strategy against the Turks. He realised the need to possess a powerful navy if he was to have any real success against the forces of Islam. The next few years were to see the Spanish dockyards fully occupied in building the new fleet.

In 1563 Philip had an opportunity to test the effectiveness of the new fleet against the Barbary pirates who were besieging the North African town of Oran which was a Spanish outpost. The Spanish fleet was sent into action swiftly and efficiently. Here was another example of Philip acting decisively when necessary, and when he was in a position to do so. 'Let haste be made to save every possible hour', Philip wrote, 'for until the moment I see them [the ships] here, I cannot help but feel justifiable anxiety'. Oran was saved. Further successes followed. In 1565 Philip's viceroy in Naples won a victory over the Turks who were besieging the island of Malta, another important defensive position in the central Mediterranean. The victory was greeted enthusiastically by many:

1   A hundred thousand years from now, the great king Philip of Spain will still be worthy of praise and renown, and worthy that all Christendom should pray as many years for the salvation of his soul, if God have not yet already given him a seat in Paradise for
5   having so nobly delivered so many gentlemen in Malta, which was about to follow Rhodes into enemy hands.

More forceful methods were needed in 1570 because the governor of Algiers had taken Tunis from a supporter of Philip. This left the Spanish garrison at La Goleta isolated (see map page 35). The Turks were also invading the island of Cyprus. A Holy League was therefore formed in 1571, consisting of Venice, Genoa, the Pope, other Italian states and Spain, to send an expedition to help Cyprus. Such action was not a priority as far as Philip was concerned. His chief aim had been to regain Tunis and then conquer Algiers. In addition he felt suspicious of the plans of Venice and the Pope. However, not to have joined would have lost him support among the Italian states.

Eventually the fleet of the Holy League, under the supreme command of Don John of Austria, Philip's illegitimate half brother, set sail. Young and charismatic, Don John united the disparate forces under his control. The fleet sailed east across the Mediterranean and met the Turkish fleet at Lepanto near the mainland of Greece. The sides were evenly matched. But victory came to the Christians when Don John broke the enemy in the centre of their formation and the Turkish admiral was killed. This settled the battle in the Christians' favour. Thousands of Turkish soldiers and sailors were killed or taken prisoner. Most of their ships were sunk or captured.

The initial rejoicing in Christian Europe was short lived. The victory was not followed up as it was late in the campaigning year and the victors themselves had suffered serious losses in men and ships. One Venetian was complaining only a few weeks after Lepanto, 'and not so much as an inch of ground gained'. This is to undervalue the victory. Never again was a large Turkish fleet seen in the western Mediterranean. The idea in Christian Europe of the invincibility of the Turks at sea was gone, 'on that day which was so happy for Christendom because all the world then learned how mistaken it had been in believing that the Turks were invincible at sea'.

Little else changed in the following years in the Mediterranean. The Holy League broke up when Venice returned to her usual method of dealing with the Turks – negotiation rather than fighting. Tunis was retaken (1573) for a time by the Spanish fleet but was soon lost again. Philip had neither the time nor the money to do more. He was by now fully involved in dealing with the Protestant challenge in England, France, and particularly in his own inheritance of the Netherlands. And while Philip looked to Northern Europe, and turned his back on his interests in the Mediterranean, the Turks were becoming more concerned with the situation to the east and their fight against Persia. Both Spain and the Turks were therefore prepared to make peace in the Mediterranean, so a number of truces were arranged and regularly renewed during the remaining years of Philip's reign.

f) The Netherlands

Philip did not accomplish much against the Turks and their allies in North Africa mainly because of his interests elsewhere in his empire and, particularly, from 1566, his growing involvement in the affairs of the Netherlands.

Philip's decisions as to what policies to follow in the Netherlands were among the most important of his reign and were to have repercussions for Spain over the next hundred years. However, Philip's own knowledge of the states was based on little personal understanding. Under his father the Netherlands had believed themselves to be the centre of the empire. Charles had been born there and it was there that he abdicated his imperial responsibilities. Charles may have travelled to other parts of his empire frequently but those who lived in the Netherlands saw him as a ruler with genuine commitment to their wellbeing. Philip was different. Born and brought up in Spain he had paid only three visits to the Netherlands. With less of the 'common touch' than his father, he does not seem to have made a great impression while there. This lack of understanding was to lead to mistakes in his dealings with the Netherlands.

In the past, a generally held view of Philip's aims in the Netherlands was that he wished to impose despotic rule over the states and make them a base from which to force the Protestant countries in Europe to reintroduce Catholicism. Most historians now consider this too extreme a view. On the other hand, it was widely believed by contemporaries, such as the Protestant Elizabeth I of England, that this was indeed Philip's intention, and it was therefore important in motivating the way in which other countries decided to act in regard to the Netherlands. It is now generally considered that Philip had two main aims: firm government in which his rights as the ruler were protected, and ensuring the position of Catholicism.

In implementing these aims Philip made several mistakes at the beginning of his reign. He appointed his half-sister Margaret, Duchess of Parma, as his governor-general, although she had spent most of her life in Italy and had little experience or understanding of the people of the Netherlands. In addition, Philip ordered that an inner advisory council of three known supporters of centrally controlled government be set up.

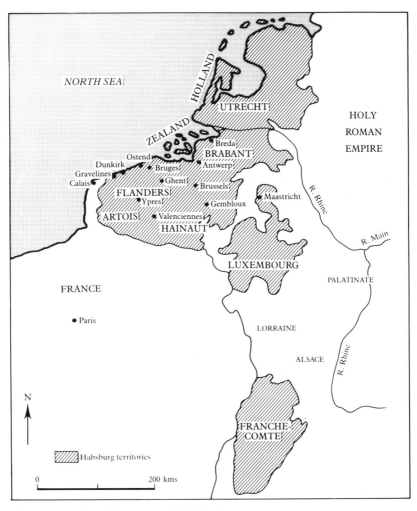

The Burgundian inheritance of Philip II

This provoked anger among the nobles in the Netherlands, particularly the rich and powerful William, Prince of Orange. These nobles felt that their position gave them the right to advise Margaret themselves and feared that an attempt was being made to introduce a more centralised government which would lead to a loss of their traditional power and prestige. Philip caused further discontent by leaving a garrison of Spanish troops behind him in the Netherlands. Although these troops were later withdrawn, many of the nobles feared that they might return and impose Spanish authority more firmly over the country.

Having angered the nobles, Philip also created antagonism over his religious policies. He planned to increase the number of bishops in the Netherlands from four to eighteen. It was argued that this would make it easier for the bishops to provide for the religious needs of the people and to deal with heresy. But, at the same time, it would increase Philip's control over the church in the Netherlands, for he himself would decide who was to be appointed to a bishopric. The Crown's political power would also be enlarged, as the bishops would all have seats in local and national assemblies. Firmer attempts were also made to deal with the growing threat of Protestantism, particularly in its more militant form of Calvinism. The Inquisition was increased in size, and further 'placards' or edicts against heresy were issued.

These policies aroused serious opposition and Philip's reactions show the working of the Spanish government at its most ineffective. Conflicting instructions were received by Margaret as to what to do, creating long delays while she awaited clarification from Madrid. Philip decided finally to make some concessions but before news of these had arrived in the Netherlands, matters there had got completely out of hand. Calvinists had rioted and seriously damaged Catholic churches – the so-called 'Iconoclastic Fury' (1566).

Philip was horrified at what had been done 'against our Lord and His images'. The methods he then adopted were, however, to lead to a far more serious outbreak of trouble. In 1567 he yielded to the advice of the Duke of Alba and sent him to the Netherlands to deal firmly with what was considered in Madrid to be a rebellion, even though, by then, Margaret seemed to have matters under control and order was being speedily restored. On Philip's instructions the Duke of Alba set up a 'Tribunal of Troubles' which sentenced over a thousand people to death for their involvement in the 1566 riots and disturbances. However, what was crucial in stirring up further trouble were Alba's orders from Philip to obtain money from the Netherlands to pay for the army. To do this Alba tried to introduce a 10 per cent tax on sales, the 'Tenth Penny'. Unrest aroused by this led to the second and more important outbreak of rebellion. By 1572 large areas of the northern Netherlands, particularly Holland and Zealand, were in revolt against Philip, led by William of Orange.

The conflict which ensued over the remaining years of Philip's reign seem to show Philip frequently unclear as to what to do about the rebellion. Alba was recalled and replaced by Luis de Requesens, who had already served Philip well both in Rome and Madrid. Requesens made concessions to the rebels but these were too late to be effective and Philip would not consider toleration of religion or a reduction in his rights as ruler. 'On these two points on no account are you to give in or shift an inch' were his orders to Requesens in 1574.

Unfortunately Requesens died in 1576 and in the intervening period before the new governor, Don John, took up his new position, attacks were made on a number of loyal towns, including Antwerp, by unpaid

An anonymous engraving on the situation in the Netherlands in the late 1560s

and starving, mutinous Spanish troops. This led to a serious escalation of the revolt. The previously loyal southern states, seeing that Spain could not protect them, joined with those of the north to expel the Spanish. On his arrival from Spain, Don John therefore had no option but to make further concessions in the Perpetual Edict of 1577. These included the withdrawal of all foreign troops from the country. However, the terms of the Edict were broken by the Calvinists in that they refused toleration of the Catholics. Fearing for his own personal safety, Don John gained Philip's agreement to call the Spanish army back to the Netherlands.

The task now was to reconquer the whole of the Netherlands, not just a few states. The army returned under the command of Alexander Farnese – the son of Philip's half-sister Margaret, Duchess of Parma (see page 71) – and a victory was won at Gembloux. In 1578 Don John died and was replaced by Farnese who had already shown his considerable political and military abilities at such battles as Lepanto. He was highly intelligent and of all Philip's governors in the Netherlands, he showed the most understanding of the problems there. He won the southern states back to Spain, convincing them that they had more to fear from an alliance with the Calvinist states than with Spain. By 1585 Maastricht, Dunkirk, Ypres, Bruges, Ghent, Ostend and Antwerp had been retaken and Farnese looked poised to secure the recovery of the remaining areas in revolt – the provinces of Holland, Zealand, and Utrecht. That he was unable to do so was probably due to two main reasons.

The first was the involvement of England officially in the war. Help had been given to the rebels from the Protestant states in Germany, England and France from the early stages of the revolt. Most of the help had been unofficial. However, in 1585, Elizabeth I signed the Treaty of Nonesuch with the rebels, agreeing to give them military aid. Though little, it was enough to support their resistance to Farnese.

More critical to Farnese were the decisions Philip took in regard to his relations with England and France. In 1585 when Farnese seemed at the point of reconquering the whole of the Netherlands, Philip decided that to do so must involve an invasion of England first. For two vital years, 1586 and 1587, Farnese was unable to fight in the Netherlands while he waited for the armada to sail so that his troops could be taken over to England. Possibly even more important was Philip's decision to intervene in the affairs of France. In 1589 Farnese was ordered to enter France to fight alongside the Catholic rebels who were attempting to prevent the legitimate, but Protestant, Henry IV becoming king (see page 79). These events gave the Calvinist rebels in the Netherlands time to improve their defences and to make several important gains. Farnese himself died in 1592.

By the end of his reign Philip must have recognised his failures in the Netherlands. By 1592 the Calvinists had both France and England as their allies. Philip was also in further financial difficulties, declaring another bankruptcy in 1596. He was therefore forced to halt his campaign against the rebels. A new approach was attempted. Philip's daughter, Isabella, was given the Netherlands to rule with her husband, the Archduke Albert. Philip hoped that if he separated the Netherlands from the rest of his empire there would eventually be a reunion of all the states. But this plan failed. The northern states were by now a clearly distinct country that was already being referred to as the United Provinces (Holland). They would not be prepared to give up their political or religious independence for which many had fought so hard for so long.

Philip's failure to defeat the rebels in the Netherlands must have appeared an impossibility at the beginning of the disturbances in the 1560s. Then, Spain, with her able commanders, her experienced fighting troops and her money from the Indies must have seemed unbeatable. What then led to Spain's failures in the Netherlands? Some of these factors have already been mentioned: Philip's own hesitation and delays, his refusal to compromise on religion and his decision to involve his forces in England and France. The involvement of foreign countries gave the rebels support at critical times. Other factors must also be considered. The beliefs of the Calvinists helped stiffen their resistance. Geographical factors played an important part. There were delays and difficulties in sending men and money either overland or by sea to the Netherlands. Once there, fighting in the north was extremely difficult. Holland was 'the Great Bog of Europe', and comprised many islands separated from the mainland by the sea. To take each town usually required long sieges.

Philip's lack of resources was crucial. He did not have the means to fight effectively in more than one part of his empire at any one time. In the early stages of the rebellion Philip was having to direct his resources against the threat of Islam in the Mediterranean. It was only during periods when he could turn away from this threat that adequate resources could be sent to the Netherlands. From the 1580s, as we have seen, Philip also decided to fight first England and then France.

The most vital resource which Philip lacked was money. It was the need for money which led Alba to propose the 'Tenth Penny' which was a significant trigger in leading to a renewal of the revolt in 1572. And Alba was unable to deal with the revolt effectively as Philip could not send him enough money between 1570 and 1574. Things became even worse in 1576 when Philip repudiated all his debts. The bankruptcy meant that he was not able to send any money to the Netherlands to pay the troops, and this led to the mutinies which frightened the loyal Catholic states of the south into joining with the northern states, and united the whole of the Netherlands against him. What could be achieved when Spain's resources were concentrated on defeating the rebels is illustrated by Farnese's successes between 1578 and 1585.

4 Relations with England

Relations between Spain and England before Philip's reign had generally been cordial. To Spain, England presented a useful ally against her traditional enemy France. In 1554 Philip had married Mary I of England and had become, in title only, King of England. But he had not been popular in England and anti-Spanish feeling grew considerably there when Spain involved England in war against France. Following the death of Mary in 1558, her half-sister, Elizabeth I, succeeded to the throne. Philip was eager to maintain good relations, even though Elizabeth was considered by many to be a Protestant. This was mainly because he did not wish to see Mary, Queen of Scots, Elizabeth's closest relative, become Queen of England, even though she was a Catholic. Mary had close links with France and Philip feared that as Queen of England, she might well form an alliance with France against Spain. Philip therefore supported Elizabeth at the beginning of her reign, offering her his hand in marriage and preventing the Pope from excommunicating her in 1561.

Relations between the two countries, however, were to become less friendly as England came to consider herself as the protector of Protestantism in Europe. This involved her in the affairs of the Netherlands. She also wished to participate in the trade of the Indies. Thus she came into conflict with Spain in two important areas of her empire.

English merchants attempted to trade with the Indies either through smuggling or, when this failed, by piracy. A major exploit was Francis Drake's round the world expedition of 1576–81, when he seized large quantities of Spanish treasure. It was no secret that Elizabeth had given her unofficial support to Drake and this served to increase tension between the two countries.

It was, however, the earlier arrival of Alba in the Netherlands in 1567 which most seriously affected relations with England, and led to the eventual outbreak of war. Elizabeth feared a Spanish presence only a few miles from England's own shores. In addition England had close economic and religious links with the growing numbers of Protestants in the Netherlands. In 1568 Elizabeth confiscated Spanish ships on their way to the Netherlands. These had had to land in England because of storms at sea. They had been carrying wool and money to pay for the Spanish troops in the Netherlands. From the early 1570s Elizabeth also provided help to the rebels in the Netherlands. She lent money to them, and paid for mercenaries to be sent there.

Official war became a certainty in 1585. Philip seized all English ships in Spanish ports in retaliation for English piracies in the West Indies. In the Netherlands, Farnese's successes made it seem likely that all of the states would once again come firmly under Spanish rule. Elizabeth feared that if the Netherlands were to be defeated Philip would decide to invade the only major Protestant country remaining in Europe, England. Elizabeth's chief minister made the point, 'If he [Philip] once reduce the Low

Countries to absolute subjection, I know not what limits any man of judgment can set unto his greatness'. Convinced of the dangers to England, Elizabeth signed the Treaty of Nonesuch with the rebels, agreeing to send about 6000 soldiers and to lend them more money. The following year, 1586, she sent an English army.

The signing of the treaty spurred Philip into taking action against England. He ordered that an armada (a fleet of warships) be prepared and made ready for an invasion of England. Some of Philip's councillors, including Alba, did not feel such an attack would work. Philip and the majority of his councillors did. It has been suggested by some historians that Philip, now nearly 60 years old, was aware that his life might soon end and wished to lead a religious crusade on behalf of Catholicism against the Protestant Elizabeth before it was too late. On the other hand the dating of the change in his policy, 1586, coming as it did after news of incidents in the West Indies and the Treaty of Nonesuch, leads most historians to believe that political and economic considerations lay at the back of his thinking. Certainly that is what the Pope thought. He made the point that Philip was motivated by considerations of 'global strategy and revenge'.

However, the armada of 1588 failed in its attempt to invade England. More than half the ships sent were destroyed and 15 000 men died. For Spain this was a serious defeat but not a decisive one. Philip had been unable to break the alliance of the English with the rebels in the Netherlands and to invade England. But the failure did not put a complete end to such plans. Philip was able to build further armadas and attempts were made to invade Ireland, always a useful base from which to attack England, in 1596 and 1598. A further armada was sent against England directly in 1597. This too failed; scattered by the weather. The war was to drag on and continue until after Philip's death.

5 France

Towards the end of his reign Philip's attention was turned principally to France rather than to England. When Philip came to the throne Spain had been at war with France. In spite of victories at St. Quentin and Gravelines the Spanish had not been able to defeat France decisively. Philip's financial difficulties at the time were serious and he had been ready to make peace in the Treaty of Cateau Cambresis (1559). In order to cement the peace, a marriage had taken place between Philip and Elizabeth of Valois, daughter of King Henry II of France.

After 1559, there was peace between France and Spain for some years. However, Philip became increasingly anxious about the growth in the number of Protestants in France. In 1562 the French wars of religion broke out, led by the Catholic family of Guise against their rivals for political power, the mainly Protestant Bourbon family. Philip's natural inclination during these wars was to support the Catholic cause, a feeling that was reinforced by fears that if France became Protestant she would present a serious danger both to the Netherlands on her north-eastern frontier and to Spain on her south-west frontier.

It was only in the 1580s that Philip decided to intervene directly in the struggle. In 1584 Henry of Navarre, a Huguenot, became heir to the French throne. This was a setback to Philip's hopes. It could have possibly led to the triumph of Protestantism in France and also to the implementation of an anti-Spanish policy. Philip decided he must prevent Henry becoming king. He therefore signed the Treaty of Joinville with the French Catholic League, headed by the Guise family. In this he promised the League financial help, and both sides agreed to support each other in defending Catholicism. Five years later Henry III was assassinated, leaving Henry of Navarre as his successor. In 1590, and again in 1592, Philip ordered Farnese to intervene in France from the Netherlands to prevent Henry becoming king. Spanish troops were also sent into Brittany. At the same time Philip put forward the claims to the French throne of Isabella, his eldest daughter by his marriage to Elizabeth of Valois. Her succession would ensure a Catholic ruler on the throne of France and bring the country under Spanish influence.

Philip's plans failed. The French were only prepared to accept a Frenchman as king. When, in 1595, Henry IV became a Catholic, most of France joined him to expel the Spanish forces. A brief war ensued. But neither side could achieve complete victory. However, when Philip became bankrupt for the third time in 1596, he decided that he must make peace. The Treaty of Vervins (1598) which ended the war confirmed the main clauses of the Treaty of Cateau Cambresis.

Little had been achieved by Philip in France, although some historians have argued that his intervention preserved Catholicism there by forcing Henry IV to change his religion. This is now considered unlikely. Of more consequence was the effect of the intervention on Philip's policies in the Netherlands. Troops needed to ensure victory there had been sent into France and this may be said to have contributed significantly to Philip's failure in the Netherlands at the end of his reign.

6 Conclusion

On his death in 1598, at the age of 71, Philip had ruled over his empire for 42 years. How far had he achieved what he had set out to do in 1556, when his main aims seem to have been protecting and maintaining his empire, preserving and defending Catholicism, and ensuring good and just government in his lands?

Philip handed on to his son the territories that he had himself received from Charles I and more. He had brought about the union of all the kingdoms in the Iberian Peninsula when he inherited Portugal. He had also acquired the vast Portuguese overseas empire made up in theory of Brazil, most of Africa, India, China, Japan and Indonesia. In practice, of course, Portugal merely attempted to retain exclusive trading rights in those areas; very rarely was any effort made to rule over them. In addition his reign had seen the extension of the Spanish Empire in America. However, though still in theory part of his empire, in practice, Philip had lost the northern states of the Netherlands by the end of his reign, and his instructions to his son not to give up his rights to any part of the empire were to create considerable difficulties for his descendants.

Philip's success in religious matters was varied. He had certainly kept Protestantism out of the states which made up his empire, apart from the northern part of the Netherlands. Within the peninsula, a revolt by the *moriscos* had been firmly put down, although his policies did not solve the religious and political threat the *moriscos* represented. Philip had won significant victories against the forces of Islam, especially at Malta and Lepanto. However, his success was not complete and the last years of his reign saw him making truces with the Turks, and the continuance of raids by Barbary pirates along the Spanish coasts.

Philip's foreign wars against England and France expended considerable sums of money with little result, and in the process they exhausted Castile. The majority of the cost of the Empire had fallen on Castile and by the end of Philip's reign signs of depression in agriculture and industry were already apparent. In addition, the financial burden that Philip left to his son was considerable.

Yet one must not exaggerate Philip's failures. Philip was the ruler of a vast empire, and for most of his reign the majority of his peoples seem to have been generally content with his rule. The despatch sent by the Venetian ambassador on Philip's death gives a final verdict in his favour:

1   The king is dead. . . . Although change is usually popular, yet
    nobles and people, rich and poor, universally show great grief. . . .
    He was a prince who fought with gold rather than with steel, by his
    brain rather than by his arms. He has acquired more by sitting still,
5   by negotiation, by diplomacy, than his father did by armies and by
    war. He was one of the richest princes the world has ever seen, yet
    he has left the revenues of the kingdom and of the crown burdened
    with about a million of debts. He owes to his good fortune rather
    than to the terror of his name the important kingdom of Portugal,
10 with all its territories and treasure; on the other hand, he has lost
    Flanders. . . . Profoundly religious, he loved peace and quiet. He
    displayed great calmness, and professed himself unmoved in good
    or bad fortune alike. He had vast schemes in his head: witness his
    simultaneous attack on England and on France, . . . while facing
15 the revolution in Flanders. . . On great occasions, in the conduct
    of wars, in feeding the civil war in France, in the magnificence of
    his buildings, he never counted the cost; he was no close reckoner,
    but lavished his gold without a thought; but in small matters, in the
    government of his household, he was more parsimonious than

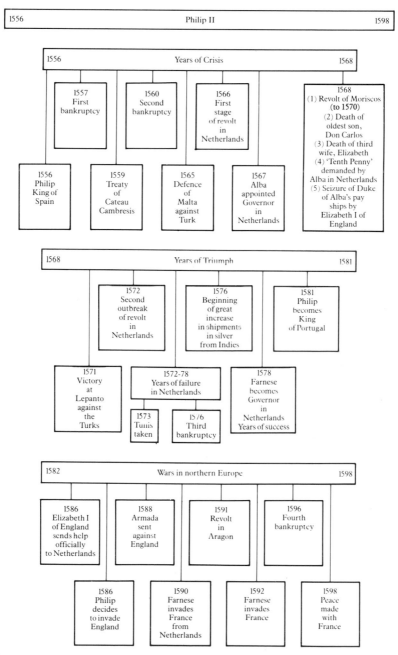

| 1556 | Philip II | 1598 |

| 1556 | Years of Crisis | 1568 |

| 1557 First bankruptcy | 1560 Second bankruptcy | 1566 First stage of revolt in Netherlands | 1568 (1) Revolt of Moriscos (to 1570) (2) Death of oldest son, Don Carlos (3) Death of third wife, Elizabeth (4) 'Tenth Penny' demanded by Alba in Netherlands (5) Seizure of Duke of Alba's pay ships by Elizabeth I of England |

| 1556 Philip King of Spain | 1559 Treaty of Cateau Cambresis | 1565 Defence of Malta against Turk | 1567 Alba appointed Governor in Netherlands |

| 1568 | Years of Triumph | 1581 |

| 1572 Second outbreak of revolt in Netherlands | 1576 Beginning of great increase in shipments in silver from Indies | 1581 Philip becomes King of Portugal |

| 1571 Victory at Lepanto against the Turks | 1572-78 Years of failure in Netherlands | 1578 Farnese becomes Governor in Netherlands Years of success |

| 1573 Tunis taken | 1576 Third bankruptcy |

| 1582 | Wars in northern Europe | 1598 |

| 1586 Elizabeth I of England sends help officially to Netherlands | 1588 Armada sent against England | 1591 Revolt in Aragon | 1596 Fourth bankruptcy |

| 1586 Philip decides to invade England | 1590 Farnese invades France from Netherlands | 1592 Farnese invades France | 1598 Peace made with France |

Summary – Philip II, 1556–98

20 became his station. He held his desires in absolute control and
showed an immutable and unalterable temper. He has feigned
injuries, and feigned not to feel injuries, but he never lost the
opportunity to avenge them. . . . No one ever saw him in a rage,
being always patient, phlegmatic, temperate, melancholy. In
25 short, he has left a glorious memory of his royal name, which may
serve as an example, not only unto his posterity and his successors,
but unto strangers as well. . . .

Making notes on 'Philip II, 1556–1598'

In making your notes on Philip II always remember, for each section, to
consider:
a) the problems faced by Philip and the constraints within which he was
   trying to rule
b) the aims that Philip himself was trying to implement
c) the extent to which he was successful
Remember too that Philip's reign lasted many years. Policies and
approaches did not all remain the same over this time. Try to bring out
these changes when making your notes.

The first thing to do is to make your own time chart to show how the
events described separately in the chapter related to one another. The
chart could include columns with the following headings: Date; Indies;
Aragon; Moriscos; Portugal; Mediterranean; Netherlands; England;
France. Keep this chart by you, and refer to it whenever you are
considering Philip's success, or otherwise, in one of his policies. You will
then see what was happening in other parts of Philip's empire at the same
time, and will be able to judge how far events were interrelated. You
could also add an extra column headed 'finance' to show the years in
which Philip went bankrupt.

The following headings and sub-headings will provide a structure for
your notes:
1.   Background
1.1. Birth
1.2. Education
1.3. Character
1.4. Preparation for kingship
2.   Method of government
2.1. Personal involvement, including advantages and disadvantages
2.2. Conciliar system
2.3. Use of secretaries
2.4. Juntas
2.5. Finance – include information on the methods Philip used to meet
      his financial commitments and how far they were successful

---

Answering essay questions on 'Philip II, 1556–1598'

Many of the essay questions you are likely to meet will involve a general assessment of Philip's aims:

> 'How far did concern for the Catholic religion influence Philip's policies?'
>
> 'Discuss Philip II's aims.'

Use the note headings and sub-headings to make a list of the topics you need to include for each of these questions. Once you have listed these, jot down Philip's aims with regard to each. Consider in what ways religion was a factor for each one. Try to decide which were the main factors which influenced Philip's policies? Did they differ at different points in his reign according to the circumstances in which he had to make decisions? Did his judgement become less good as he became older? Your conclusion could offer some answer to the last two points.

Some essay questions go further than this and ask why Philip had difficulties in accomplishing his aims:

'How far did the size of his empire prevent Philip II achieving his aims?'

Here the question gives you some help in indicating one aspect to consider – the size of Philip's empire – and you should include all the evidence you can which relates to this. Of course, you will then need to deal with other factors which prevented Philip achieving his aims. Here such aspects as Philip's method of governing the empire and his financial position will need to be considered.

A number of questions involve discussion of Philip's success or otherwise as a ruler:

'How successful a ruler was Philip II?'

Again, list the topics you would wish to include and for *each*, note in what ways, if any, Philip was successful. Make a similar list of the ways he was unsuccessful. Do you need to make a distinction between short-term and long-term success? Then decide the most effective order in which to present your points. Should you use the strongest argument first, or should you save it to last?

Source-based questions on 'Philip II, 1556–1598'

1   The character of Philip II
Read the extracts on pages 54–5 and look at the picture on page 56, then answer the following questions:
a)   What do these extracts and the portrait suggest about Philip's character?
b)   In what ways are ambassadors' reports, such as the first extract, useful as historical sources?
c)   What shortcomings, as evidence about his character, are revealed in Philip's letters to his daughters?
d)   Discuss the usefulness and the limitations to historians of this period of portraits such as this of Philip II.
e)   What other evidence would you wish to study to gain a full picture of Philip's character?

2   Philip and Aragon
Read the document on pages 63–4 and answer the following questions:
a)   What does this extract reveal of the difficulties involved in governing Aragon?
b)   How far does this assessment explain i) why Philip did not involve himself in the affairs of Aragon during the early part of his reign; ii) the reasons why he did so after 1580?

3   The Netherlands in the late 1560s

Look carefully at the engraving on page 74. In it the Duke of Alba has a helmet on his head and the Prince of Orange is bareheaded. Answer the following questions:

a)   Who were the Duke of Alba and the Prince of Orange?
b)   Explain carefully, referring to the engraving, what the engraver's attitude is to i) Alba and ii) Orange. What does this tell you about the engraver and whom he intended this picture to be seen by?
c)   Using your own knowledge, assess how far the engraver is making an accurate statement about Alba's policies in the Netherlands.

4   The death of Philip

Read the extract on pages 80–2 carefully and answer the following questions:

a)   What does the writer consider to be i) the successful features and ii) the unsuccessful features of Philip's reign?
b)   What impression do you gain of Philip's character from this extract? How far does it agree with the extracts in question 1? How could you explain any differences you find?
c)   How credible do you find this account? Give reasons for your answer.

CHAPTER 5

The Decline of Spain? 1598–1643

During the first quarter of the seventeenth century a number of contemporaries within Spain expressed anxieties about the state of her society, her economy and her international position.

Criticism came from all directions. Complaints were made in the Cortes, from the pulpits, by state advisers, by ordinary people protesting in public and by political writers. One influential group of writers were known as the *arbitristas*. They were professional people such as lawyers, clergy and state officials who wrote mainly on the economic problems of the time. They gave both an assessment of what they felt was wrong with Spain, and offered suggestions (*arbitrios*) on how the problems might be solved.

Many comments concerned Spanish society itself. Typical attacks were on issues such as sexual immorality, the idleness of the young, luxurious living (especially eating and drinking too much), and even the fashion among men of wearing long hair. This was considered by some to be effeminate. The extremes of wealth were also criticised.

In economic affairs the complaints included the poor state of the Crown's finances, the tax burden on peasants, the fact that more goods were coming into the country for sale than were going out as exports, the presence of many foreign merchants selling their goods in Spain, the decline of Spain's own domestic industry, and the problems created by the *vellon* coinage (coins which were debased or lowered in value by being made of a mixture of copper and silver rather than pure silver or pure gold). However, most alarming was the fall in population. In 1600 one commentator wrote:

> Never in seven hundred years of continuous war, nor in a hundred of continuous peace, has Spain as a whole been as ruined and as poor as it is now.

In addition, from the 1620s, there were many complaints about a decline in both Spain's international position and her status as a military power. In particular, it was felt that there was too much involvement in the Netherlands and that interests in the Mediterranean should again take priority over those in northern Europe. Some rejected the idea that Spain should be part of a great empire. One depressing remark of the time was that

> it has cost a great deal to wage war in inhospitable and remote provinces, at the price of so much life and money, and with such great benefit to the enemy and so little to us that it may be asked whether we would not be better conquered than conquering.

Complaints were also made that the burden of defending the empire fell mainly on Castile:

1   All monarchies have been accustomed to enrich the head of the empire with the spoils and tributes of provinces and nations won by arms or legitimately acquired by other means. . . . Only Castile has pursued a different method of government, because, while it
5   should, as the head, be the most privileged in the payment of taxes, it is in fact the most heavily taxed of all, and contributes the largest sum to the Monarchy's defence. . . . It is only reasonable that the burdens should be distributed in proper proportion: that Castile should continue to provide for the royal household and for
10   the defence of its own coasts and the routes to the Indies; that Portugal should pay for its own garrisons and for the East Indies fleets, as it did before it was incorporated with Castile, and that Aragon and Italy should defend their coasts and maintain the necessary militia and ships for the purpose. It is quite unreasonable
15   that the head should be weakened while the other members, which are very rich and populous, should simply stand by and look on while it has to bear all these heavy charges.

The picture painted by many contemporaries was a depressing one, although no more so than could have been painted of almost every European country at the time. The views expressed have, however, been generally accepted by historians until recently. Now that more of the primary evidence, especially on political and military affairs, has been carefully studied by historians, traditional views of the position of Spain during the early seventeenth century are being modified.

1 Philip III, 1598–1621

One of the areas in which historians are revising their assessments is in the abilities of the rulers of Spain during this period. These rulers (Philip III, Philip IV and, though outside the scope of this work, Charles II) have traditionally been viewed as complete incompetents who bore a major responsibility for the decline of Spain. This interpretation has been challenged by some historians.

Philip III was twenty when he succeeded his father in 1598. The commonly held view of him has been that he was 'the laziest king in Spanish history . . . frivolous, incompetent . . . a disaster', who was willing to leave government in the hands of others. Historians such as Kamen now see him in a somewhat more positive way, particularly in his attempts to make government more efficient and to improve the military position of the country.

Under Philip III the style of government changed. He did not wish to govern as his father had done, with the king exercising personal control over much of the work, and using his secretaries as intermediaries between himself and the councils. Instead, he appointed a chief minister, usually known as a *valido*. It was with him that Philip would consult on the papers and advice he was sent. The *valido*'s power depended on his personal friendship with the king. To keep power he needed to maintain that support.

The traditional view of the creation of this position is that it was a symptom of Spain's decline. The king was opting out of fulfilling his responsibilities. He was finding someone else to do the necessary work so that he could devote his time to his pleasures. This view must now be somewhat modified. Several historians have pointed out that, by Philip's reign, if not before, the amount of government business was so enormous that it was impossible for any one man to deal with it. To share the burden was a sensible approach to dealing with the problems of government. It was Philip II's way of working which had created dangers for the government of the Empire:

> If His Majesty [Philip II] should tire of working – as at present – and want to take some day for himself, or if illness should so oblige him, the whole machine [of government] is brought to a standstill.

Philip's first *valido* was the Duke of Lerma, whose main concern seems to have been to revive the financial position of his family and to increase its social standing among the nobility. It is estimated that, by the end of the reign, Lerma's fortune stood at around three million ducats. Friends and relatives had gained positions at court and in the government, and his children had married into the most prestigious aristocratic families.

Wherever the king went so did Lerma. This might mean that the two spent months away from Madrid. As a result neither regularly played a very active part in the detailed government of Spain. A split took place between the Court, which travelled with the king, and the administration, which remained in Madrid. In practice, government was delegated to the councils.

Philip seems to have been personally responsible for the changes to the conciliar system which were aimed at making it more effective and able to work without the king's presence in Madrid. The Council of State met regularly and dealt with the major issues of the day. The Council of War also began to meet regularly. And the Council of Finance which, at the beginning of the reign, had even had difficulty in providing the food for Philip's own table, was reformed so that it too met more frequently and was required to be more accountable for its work.

More business went to the councils. Costs doubled as the numbers of administrators increased. But the additional work-load was too large for them to carry. As a result, juntas continued to be established to deal with specific matters as they had been under Philip II. In the past, historians have seen this, probably unfairly, as an example of decline in the standards of government. Juntas had, as we have seen (page 59), existed under Philip II, and were an efficient way of dealing with specific problems quickly.

Historians have also traditionally criticised the abilities of the men appointed to the administration under Philip III. Some of those who had served under Philip II were dismissed and those who replaced them were seen as inferior in quality and as only being appointed because of the patronage of Lerma. Control of patronage meant that Lerma decided who received rewards and offices. One Venetian ambassador's words have been influential in shaping this opinion:

1   I say that in Spain the Council [of State] is everything, but it is not free, except in name, for there is no one who dares give his view freely, and especially so if it is against the will of the Duke [of Lerma]. For having done so, Garcia de Loaysa, Archbishop of
5   Toledo . . . fell into disgrace and Rodrigo Vezquez, president of Castile, was stripped of his duties and expelled from the Court, [and this] cost him his life. The same thing happened to . . . the inquisitor general and to . . . , [a] gentlemen of the chamber, who spoke ill of the Duke [Lerma] to the king. In matters of state . . .
10   there is a division between the followers of Philip II and those of Philip III, each holding superior the government of his time.

However, it should be noted that the men named in this report were either old or not of any particular ability. It is therefore not surprising that replacements should be found for them. Any new regime must be expected to make some new appointments. Those of men like the Duke of Alba and the Duke of Infantado to the Council of State were appointments of men of ability chosen because of their proven competence in service to the Crown. In addition, this particular ambassador was not even present in Spain during this time. Another contemporary, an enemy of Lerma's, wrote:

The King, on inheriting these kingdoms, established a great council of state, and appointed to it great men, all very well qualified, each of them worthy of governing the whole world.

There were still some ministers who continued to serve Philip as they had done his father. One of Philip II's most able and efficient administrators, Idiaquez, continued to be an influential voice on Philip III's Councils.

Towards the end of Philip's reign further governmental changes were made. Lerma lost the confidence of the king in 1618 and was dismissed. His successor as *valido* was his son, Cristobel, Duke of Uceda. This time, however, Philip retained control over both government and patronage. Papers were in future only to be signed by himself. Then Philip died unexpectedly in 1621.

a) The Expulsion of the *Moriscos*

One of the major events of the reign of Philip III, and one for which he has been most criticised, was the expulsion of the *moriscos* in 1609. The Council of State had first proposed such an expulsion in 1582. However, there were objections to it from those areas of Spain where large groups of *moriscos* were still to be found. The nobles of Aragon and Valencia needed the *moriscos* as tenants and as workers on their estates and did not wish to see them leave the country.

The decision to expel the *moriscos* seems to have come as a surprise to most people in Spain. Even the Council of State was divided over the issue. There was no demand from the Cortes of either Castile or the Crown of Aragon for such a policy. The major political writers of the period were against it.

Various suggestions have been put forward by historians to explain why the expulsion took place when it did. One recent historian attributed it mainly to the fact that Lerma changed his mind. From being opposed to expulsion he declared his support for it. Part of his reason for doing so seems to have been that he wished to see the lands of the *moriscos* given to Valencian nobles in recompense for the loss of their *morisco* workers. He himself, as the owner of estates in Valencia, would naturally receive additional land. And we know that, above all else, he was determined to increase his personal wealth. Other historians have seen the expulsion as an attempt to gain popularity among the ordinary people, particularly in Castile, by expelling a group long held to be their traditional enemy. The move would also serve to distract attention from the Twelve Years Truce recently signed with the Dutch, which might not be viewed very favourably by many Spanish.

Other more general factors were also involved. The Archbishop of Valencia urged the expulsion because of the problems he was encountering in making the *moriscos* into genuine converts to Christianity. There were also reports that the *moriscos* were in contact with the French. Fear of an uprising, therefore, considerably concerned the government.

The decree for the expulsion of the *moriscos* from Valencia was passed on 4 April 1609. They were ordered to leave the kingdom by September. The expulsion was then extended to other parts of Spain. Over a five year period about 300 000 out of the 320 000 *moriscos* living in Spain left. Most ended up in North Africa. The writer Cervantes makes one of his *morisco* characters support Philip's act 'to expel poisonous fruit from Spain, now clean and free of the fears to which our numbers held her'. The *moriscos* themselves spoke of the expulsion as if they were being sent out of their homeland, 'wherever we are we weep for Spain, for we were born there and it is our native land'.

The action was quickly regretted by the government. The sufferings of those expelled, many of whom were robbed or died from the hardships experienced on the march to the ports, were condemned both within Spain and in other European countries as 'this most barbarous act in the annals of mankind'. The effects on Spain varied from area to area. Certain towns in Castile such as Toledo, Cordoba and Seville suffered from the loss of a significant proportion of their working population. Most severely hit, however, were Valencia and Aragon. In Valencia 30 per cent of the population had gone, in Aragon 20 per cent. Agricultural output dropped, rents and taxes fell. The Valencian and Aragonese nobles suffered considerable financial loss. Attempts were made to encourage people to come to Valencia from other parts of Spain in order to make up some of the loss, but by 1700 only about a thousand such settlers had arrived.

2 Philip IV, 1621–65

The death of Philip III in 1621 at the early age of 42 left as king his 16 year old son, Philip IV. As with Philip III, historians have recently modified the traditional view of Philip IV, particularly over his attitude to involvement in the work of government. The accepted view of Philip used to be that he was 'weak and lazy', 'with a lust for pleasure which he was powerless to resist' and which 'made him the slave of favourites and his passions all his life'. Such a picture is probably too extreme. Philip seems to have grown into a conscientious ruler. Certainly, many comments in his own hand were made on the *consultas* (reports summarising what took place at each meeting of a council) presented to him.

Philip IV comes over as a warmer, more human, personality than the previous two Philips. He was intelligent, pious and caring, and he extensively supported the arts, particularly drama. His major defect seems to have been his lack of confidence, which led him to depend on others. One contemporary expressed the view that Philip 'would be capable of governing under any conditions, were it not that he mistrusts himself and defers too much to others'. This was especially so at the beginning of his reign, when the most important influence was Gaspar de Guzman, Count of Olivares.

a) Olivares

Olivares was 34 years old when he took over the affairs of government soon after Philip's accession to the throne in 1621. He was forceful, dynamic, energetic, and intellectually able. He pushed the young Philip into work even when the latter was reluctant, 'the problems of government are such that your Majesty cannot evade assuming your share of the burden, under pain of grave and mortal sin'. He was concerned with political power not, like Lerma, with personal gain. In many ways Olivares was an ideal statesman. He worked hard, understood the detailed working of government, particularly finance, and was completely honest. Unfortunately he also exhibited faults which were eventually to prove crucial. He disliked criticism, and, once set on a policy, he was reluctant to change his mind. This meant that he was seldom prepared to abandon even those policies which had little chance of success. A Venetian ambassador gave a revealing view of him:

1   He loves novelties, allowing his lively mind to pursue chimeras,
    and to hit upon impossible designs as easy of achievement. For this
    reason, he is desolated by misfortunes; the difficulties proposed to
    him at the beginning he brushes aside, and all his resolutions rush
5   him towards the precipice.

Under Olivares's enthusiastic leadership at the beginning of the reign
it seemed that improvements might be made to Spain's financial and
economic position. A *Junta da Reformation* was set up in 1622 to get rid
of 'vices, abuses and bribes'. Economies were made such as in the
expenses of the court. Attempts were made to stop foreign imports
coming into the country and to encourage investment in agriculture and
industry. Measures to halt the inflation of the period were also
introduced (see page 102–3).

Olivares's vision extended beyond such measures. In a secret memo-
randum to the king in 1625 he expressed his wish to see all parts of the
Empire brought together with each kingdom contributing to the costs as
well as receiving the benefits of such a vast collection of lands.

1   Let your Majesty hold as the most important affair of your State to
    make yourself King of Spain. I mean, Sire, that you should not
    content yourself with being King of Portugal, of Aragon, of
    Valencia, Count of Barcelona, but that you should strive and
5   consider with mature and secret counsel to reduce these realms of
    which Spain consists to the laws and form of Castile, without any
    distinction. If your Majesty succeeds in this, you will be the most
    powerful Prince in the world. . . . What reason is there that these
    [non-Castilian] vassals should be excluded from honour or
10 privilege in these kingdoms [of Castile]? Why should not they
    equally enjoy the honours, offices and confidence given to those
    born in the heart of Castile and Andalusia? . . . Is it surprising
    that, with these Castilian vassals being admitted to all the
    honourable positions round Your Majesty, and enjoying the royal
15 presence, there should be jealousy, and discontent and distrust?
    There is the greatest justification for discontent in those other
    kingdoms and provinces, which have not only put up with
    government for so many years without the presence of the king,
    but are also regarded as unfitted for honours and unequal to the
20 other vassals. . . .

Olivares seemed to have recognised the resentment of Castilians at
having to bear the major costs of empire, and also the complaints of the
non-Castilians that they were excluded from all the offices, posts and
rewards. However, his one and only attempt to implement these ideas,
the Union of Arms of 1625 (see below page 94) met with almost total
failure. Olivares did not understand that such ideas might only confirm

the suspicions of the non-Castilian kingdoms that they were being 'Castilianised', and therefore would be strongly resisted.

In spite of his failure over the Union of Arms and of his ideas on bringing the Empire into far closer unity, by 1627 there was a real possibility that Olivares might succeed in improving Spain's financial position and secure necessary reforms. However, any such opportunity was thrown away. As will be seen below, in 1628 Olivares decided to support an intervention in Mantua and this was a major cause of the war which broke out with France in 1635. War meant the need for more money. However, by then virtually no silver shipments were arriving from the Indies. Spain's finances were in complete disarray. Even Castile could pay no more taxes. Desperate attempts by Olivares to raise money from other parts of the empire provoked major revolts in Catalonia and Portugal, which in their turn involved further expense.

By 1640, therefore, Olivares's policies had ended in complete failure, partly through his own unrealistic expectations of what he could achieve, partly through the difficult economic circumstances of the period, including a lack of finance and a lack of manpower. Intrigue at court and Olivares's own mental state led to his receiving permission from Philip to retire to his estates and it was there that he died two years later.

In his place, for most of the rest of the reign, power lay in the hands of Olivares's nephew, Luis de Haro. Although he had the powers of a *valido*, his title was that of 'first minister', and he never enjoyed the same authority as Olivares had done. Philip IV gave more personal attention to state affairs, and, after Haro's death in 1661, conducted the government himself for the remaining four years of his life.

3 The Empire and Foreign Policy

One of Olivares's main concerns was to preserve the Spanish Empire intact. This presented serious problems. France, England and the Dutch were all trying to gain parts of Spain's vast overseas empire. In the early seventeenth century, France, in particular, became of considerable political, economic and military importance and was eager to attack the power of Spain wherever she could. She had the advantage of being a compact single geographical unit. In contrast, Spain's empire in Europe was far-flung and difficult to defend. However Spain's greatest burden at this time was probably the government's refusal to recognise the independence of what were effectively by now the United Provinces (Holland). Holland, as an independent country (even if not yet recognised as such by Spain), was also becoming an important political and economic power in Europe. To continue to fight her involved great expense, which in the end did not result in her re-incorporation into the Spanish Empire.

There was a brief period of peace for Spain during the early years of the reign of Philip III. Peace was made with France in 1598. In 1604 the

Treaty of London brought the war with England to an end. From then on full attention could be given to the Netherlands.

* In 1604 conditions for fighting in the Netherlands improved. More money became available as a result of an increase in the Indies trade, and the extremely able Genoese general, Ambrosio Spinola, was given charge of the campaign. This led to some successes among which was the capture of Ostend.

However, the situation soon changed. The Dutch fought back well, and not enough money could be found to pay the troops. In 1606 this led to another major mutiny by Spanish soldiers. In both Holland and Spain the supporters of peace became influential in the government, and a truce was agreed in 1609 which was to last for twelve years.

* But, before the end of Philip III's reign Spain was again involved in war in Europe. In 1618 the Thirty Years War began. This started when Bohemia rebelled against Philip's close relative, the Emperor Ferdinand II, and the latter asked Spain for help. Not wishing to let down the other branch of his family, Philip agreed to give support in a struggle against Protestants. The fact that Ferdinand agreed to give Spain the province of Alsace, which was of vital strategic importance on the 'Spanish Road' to the Netherlands, (see map page 35) also helped. In 1620, therefore, Spanish troops helped Ferdinand defeat the Bohemian rebels at the Battle of the White Mountains. Another army occupied Alsace, while a large part of the force which had been in the Netherlands under Spinola crossed the River Rhine and occupied the Palatine. This would be a useful position on the Spanish route from Italy to Flanders. When Philip III died in 1621 he therefore left his son with a new war but with an inheritance that was intact.

* The plans of Philip IV for his empire were, to start with at least, largely Olivares's plans. Olivares wanted all Spanish territories to play a full part in the protection of the empire rather than relying so heavily on Castile. To this end, he proposed a Union of Arms:

1   The only remedy for all the ills that can occur is that, as loyal
     vassals, we all unite . . . considering it certain that all the enemies
     of His Majesty will give up the struggle when they see that each of
     his kingdoms can count on the support of all the others, and that
5   they form one single body.

Each part of the empire would contribute a number of troops to a common force. This force would then be used to assist any part of the empire that was under attack. It was a good idea in theory. It would lead to mutual links between all parts of the Empire. Its major defect, however, was that for the provinces of the Empire which had contributed little or no money or troops in the past, Olivares's plan represented a major financial burden, and for this reason it failed to win general acceptance.

* War was restarted with Holland when the Twelve Years Truce came

to an end in 1621. This had seemed likely for some time, although the southern Netherlands generally wished peace to continue because of the considerable costs involved in fighting. More weight, however, was given to those in Spain who advocated war. There was considerable concern about Dutch attacks on the Portuguese areas of the empire, particularly in Brazil and it was hoped that a resumption of the war would result in the destruction of Dutch power. The majority of the Dutch themselves wished to renew the war so that there would be increased opportunities to attack Spain's overseas empire. The truce had merely given them time to prepare for further fighting.

Spain made a promising start. In 1625 the port of Bahia in Brazil was recaptured from the Dutch who had taken it the previous year. Spinola also took Breda in Holland. Using the Spanish Netherlands as a base, attacks were made against Dutch shipping, resulting in the capture of many vessels. England entered the war against Spain in 1625 but an expedition to Cadiz failed to accomplish anything. Little further was done by England and a peace treaty was finally signed in 1630.

* In 1626 the Spanish could therefore look back with pride at what they had accomplished so far. In that year Philip was full of optimism when he addressed the Council of Castile:

1 Our prestige has been immensely improved. We have had all Europe against us, but we have not been defeated, nor have our allies lost, whilst our enemies [the French] have sued me for peace. Last year, 1625, we had nearly 300 000 infantry and cavalry in our
5 pay, and over 500 000 men of the militia under arms, whilst the fortresses of Spain are being put into a thorough state of defence. The fleet, which consisted of only seven vessels on my accession, rose at one time in 1625 to 108 ships of war at sea, without counting the vessels at Flanders, and the crews are the most skilful marines
10 this realm ever possessed. Thank God, our enemies have never captured one of my ships, except a solitary hulk. So it may truly be said that we have recovered our prestige at sea; and fortunately so, for, lacking our sea power, we should lose not only all the realms we possess, but religion even in Madrid itself would be ruined, and
15 this is the principal point to be considered. This very year of 1626 we have had two royal armies in Flanders and one in the Palatinate, and yet all the power of France, England, Sweden, Venice, Savoy, Denmark, Holland, Brandenberg, Saxony and Weimer could not save Breda from our victorious arms. We have held our own against
20 England, both with regard to the marriage and at Cadiz; and yet, with all this universal conspiracy against us, I have not depleted my patrimony by 50 000 ducats. It would be impossible to believe this if I did not see it with my own eyes, and that my own realms are all quiet and religious. I have written this paper to you to show you
25 [the Council of Castile, the supreme administrative, judicial, and

financial authority in Spain] that I have done my part, and have put my own shoulder to the wheel without sparing sacrifice. I have spent nothing unnecessary upon myself, and I have made Spain and myself respected by my enemies.

* Feelings of jubilation were short-lived. In the following year Spain became involved in a war which was to be both unsuccessful and to have serious repercussions. In 1627 the Duke of Mantua died. The person with the strongest claim to succeed to his independent dukedom was French. Spain was worried that, if a supporter of France held Mantua there would be opportunities for French interference in Spanish interests in Northern Italy. The Spanish governor of Milan therefore invaded Mantua, and received the support of Olivares for his action. Olivares, optimistic as always, probably hoped for a quick victory. But, the French retaliated, and a long and expensive war ensued. It only ended in 1631 when Spain renounced all claim to the duchy. The war had been a total failure for Spain. Her armed forces had experienced a surprising military defeat. The cost of fighting the war had meant that there was now little chance of putting her finances on a firmer footing. And it brought the possibility of a major war with France much closer.

* In 1635 war with France eventually broke out. The immediate cause was the victory of the Spanish at the battle of Nordlingen in southern Germany in 1634. At this battle they had defeated the Protestant Swedes, who were then the main opponents of the Emperor, in the Thirty Years War. The French had supported the Swedes financially, and now had to enter the war themselves if they were to prevent a complete Habsburg victory. Spain had hoped to avoid war with France, especially as she was short of money. The government was experiencing severe financial difficulties as income from the Indies had fallen considerably. There were also problems in obtaining enough men to fight. France had all the advantages. She entered the war fresh and, being in a central geographical position, she was able to strike out at Spanish possessions on all sides. Spain itself was invaded, although without great success. However, France's allies took the strategically important Rhine fortress of Breisach, thus cutting the route from Milan to Flanders and leaving the Spanish troops in the Netherlands isolated.

* During this war Spanish forces suffered two defeats which have been considered to be of considerable significance by historians writing about these events. The first was the Battle of the Downs (1639) and the second was the defeat of a Spanish army at Rocroi (1643).

The Battle of the Downs took place when the Spanish fleet entered English waters after an unsuccessful attack on a Dutch fleet. The Spanish anchored near Dover. The admiral of the Dutch fleet followed and attacked, destroying a large number of Spanish vessels and men. This has traditionally been seen by historians as signifying the end of Spain's power at sea. In particular, it has been argued that this defeat meant that

Spain was no longer able to maintain a sea link with the Netherlands. Certainly there was a significant loss of Spanish ships, and a Spanish survivor described the battle as 'the worst misfortune which, without the intervention of the elements, the Spanish navy has suffered in history'. However, the admiral of the Spanish fleet managed to get some of his ships to the Netherlands, along with all the bullion the ships were carrying, and one third of the infantry. Later another third of the infantry arrived safely. Communication by sea with the Netherlands also continued into the late 1660s, even after the ports of Gravelines and Dunkirk were lost.

On land the defeat at the Battle of Rocroi in 1643 has usually been seen as the point which marks the end of Spain's military greatness. The governor of the Netherlands had invaded France and had laid siege to Rocroi. The Spanish army, consisting of mercenaries from a variety of countries as well as Spanish troops, was attacked by a French force. The Spanish, suffering from a lack of cavalry and equipment, were completely defeated. Spanish casualties were high. Only the core of the army, the Spanish troops themselves, refused to flee and stayed, prepared to fight to the death. In the end, as night fell, the French commander allowed them to leave the field of battle in freedom. Though defeated they had kept their honour. To the victors it was a moment of jubilation which was echoed by Spain's enemies throughout Europe. A psychological barrier had been removed. The Spanish were no longer thought of as the invincible force of old. But the defeat did not mark the total eclipse of Spain as a military force, and a new army was quickly recruited. Of far greater concern to Spain at this time were the problems she was experiencing within the Iberian Peninsula itself.

a) Catalonia

The Catalans had a long tradition of semi-independence, at first within the Crown of Aragon, and latterly within what was generally known as Spain. They disliked the dominance of Castile in Spanish affairs and jealously defended their rights against any imagined Castilian encroachment. They were proud of the fact that their constitution made it very difficult for the King to raise large amounts of revenue from them. Consequently they paid little towards the budget of the Spanish king. Olivares was determined to obtain more. He felt that enough money could be raised from Catalonia to support the Union of Arms. But, when he tried to implement his plans, the Catalans, who by now were feeling neglected by a king who had failed to visit them, were highly reluctant to agree to the Union. The Catalans would only have agreed if Philip had made large concessions.

When war broke out with France in 1635 Olivares was optimistic that the Catalans would help, but at first neither troops nor money were forthcoming. In 1640, however, Catalans helped to recapture the frontier fortress of Salces, losing over 4000 men in the process, including about a quarter of the Catalan aristocracy. Soldiers were now billeted in Catalonia in preparation for a new campaign. This caused uproar in Barcelona and resulted in the murder of the viceroy. The Catalans began separate negotiations with France, and in October 1640 a formal defence agreement with the French was signed. Olivares was now faced by a revolt within the Spanish peninsula. Additional money would have to be raised at a time when it was already desperately short. No wonder that Olivares himself became very depressed and dispirited.

War between France and Spain for the possession of Catalonia continued into the early 1650s when the situation changed in favour of the Spanish king. France became involved in civil war and could no longer protect Catalonia from Spanish forces. Philip IV promised the Catalans that he would respect their traditional liberties and thus gained the support of those who had come to dislike the French even more than the Castilians. In 1652 Barcelona was recovered from the French and Catalonia rejoined Spain.

b) Portugal

More serious was the revolt of Portugal in 1640. Portugal had retained control over its own affairs and over its empire since its union with Castile under Philip II. Relationships became more difficult during the reign of Philip IV mainly because of the feelings of resentment in Portugal at Spain's inability to protect the Portuguese spice trade and colonies, particularly Brazil, from Dutch attack. In addition, Olivares, who needed money to fight the war against France, tried to obtain extra taxes from the Portuguese which resulted in riots taking place in some Portuguese towns in 1637. When Portuguese forces were asked to fight in Catalonia, this was the final straw. An uprising in Lisbon in 1640 led to the proclamation of the Duke of Braganza as King John IV.

Spain could not retaliate. Her armies were involved in Catalonia. Her naval losses in the Battle of the Downs had left her without a fleet to send against Portugal. It was not until 1659 and 1665 that Spanish armies were sent to Portugal. By then it was too late. The Spanish armies were defeated and finally in 1668 Spain recognised the independence of Portugal.

That the Portuguese were able to win is not surprising. Spain had too many military commitments elsewhere and was unable to send in enough troops at an early enough stage in the rebellion to obtain victory. The Portuguese, for their part, were united in their opposition to Spain. They were also able to obtain naval and military help from France.

c) Castile

Even in Castile there was agitation among the ordinary people. A revolt took place in the Basque region (1631–2) as a result of Olivares's attempt to introduce a salt tax, but it quickly became a much more general defence of the rights of the Basques against Castilian rule. It was to last for two years until put down in 1634 by the Basques themselves. Other examples of riot and disturbances took place in Navarre (1638) and Andalucia (1647–1652). In a number of important cities risings also took place: in Toledo in 1634, Granada in 1648, and Cordoba and Seville in 1652. Most were the result of famine and hardship.

d) Foreign Policy 1643–59

Further defeats followed Rocroi (see page 97). In the Netherlands Dunkirk was lost in 1646. When the Thirty Years War ended in Germany in 1648, the Spanish Crown at last agreed to recognise the independence of the United Provinces (Holland). However, war with France continued and although France herself was entering a period of internal problems, Spain was in no position to exploit the situation. But it did allow her to regain Dunkirk, end the Catalan revolt and, in 1656, to win a victory at Valenciennes in the Netherlands, the last victory the Spanish were to win in northern Europe.

At this stage France was eager to make peace, but Philip, against the advice of his ministers, refused the opportunity. He was not prepared to accept the condition that his sole heir at the time, Maria Teresa, should marry the French king, Louis XIV, and thereby possibly bring the Spanish Empire under French rule. The war therefore dragged on, with Spain having increasing problems in defending her empire. Finally the Peace of the Pyrenees was signed with France in 1659. France gained Roussillon, Cerdagne and Artois from Spain.

4 The Economy

One of the reasons for Spain's failure in the military sphere was the difficulty of recruiting for the army in the first half of the seventeenth century when a serious decline in her population occurred. Between 1530 and 1591 the population of the Spanish kingdoms had increased, particularly in Castile, where it reached approximately 8½ million. But by 1580 it had already started to fall in many towns. Again it was Castile which was affected more than other areas of the country. By 1700 there were only about seven million people in the whole of Spain.

There were many causes of the decline in population, most of which were linked to a rise in the death rate. Natural disasters played a part in this. From 1561 onwards there was a series of poor harvests, and the resulting food shortages weakened many and left them vulnerable to diseases. Many others died of hunger. In several areas there were epidemics. The great plague of 1596–1602 affected many parts of Castile and led to the deaths of about 10 per cent of the population. There was a

'*The Knight's Dream*' *by Antonia Pereda, about 1665. An allegorical
painting showing Spain's despair at her 'decline'. The figure of death is shown
above the table.*

second devastating plague in 1647–52. Lesser epidemics of smallpox, typhus and dysentery also took their toll. Of less significance were other causes such as emigration to America, deaths on military service, and the expulsion of the *moriscos*.

* The decline in population was the cause of one of the problems in agriculture – a shortage of labour. But there were other difficulties. Only a small proportion of the country's land was suitable for growing crops. Droughts were common. Farming methods were primitive.

> We still follow the ancient method of scratching at the top soil with a plough, then letting it lie fallow for three or four years, without ever asking the real causes of sterility but attributing everything to lack of water.

The way in which land was distributed also created problems. The majority of the peasants were landless labourers. Most land was in the hands of the aristocracy, who generally had no interest in farming it efficiently. For most of them land was a sign of status in society and not something to be developed in order to produce an income or more food.

In Valencia the land had been improved through the work of the *moriscos*. Their expulsion had resulted in a serious loss of workers involved in the growing of sugar, rice and grain. One contemporary chronicler wrote that Valencia 'which was formerly the most flourishing region of Spain is now reduced to an arid and neglected desert'. The effect of this was that Spain did not produce enough grain to feed her population and money had to be spent on importing food.

In the past historians thought that a major cause of the agrarian crisis was the importance given to livestock and sheep farming at the expense of arable farming. Recent research has rendered this view unacceptable. It is now clear that during the sixteenth century expansion of farming it was in fact arable that increased, at the expense of pasture. When the depression developed, both declined. Although measures were taken in some areas of Castile to encourage the return of land to pasture, these attempts failed and the numbers of sheep declined considerably.

The peasant farmer struggled under more and more difficulties. As the population declined, those left in the villages were expected to pay the same amount in taxes as had been raised when there had been more people living there. This sometimes meant that more than half a peasant's income was taken in taxes. Many fell into debt. Most found it difficult even to feed themselves. There was little surplus cash available for the purchase of manufactured goods. Similarly, many of those who worked in the towns had to pay high prices for food and had little money to buy manufactured goods.

* Manufacturing had already started to decline in the sixteenth century. This continued into the seventeenth century. Iron production, ship-building and the main industry, woollen cloth production, all declined. There was a failure to produce goods of the quality required and also a

reluctance to invest money in industry. It was far less risky and gave a higher return to lend the money, especially to the government. The guild organisation prevented changes in working practices, and government policies did nothing to help. There were heavy taxes on manufactured goods. Customs duties had to be paid on goods between Castile, the Basque provinces, Navarre, the Aragonese kingdoms and Andalucia. In addition, there was a variety of local tolls.

A collapse did not, however, take place in all industries. Those which relied on local raw materials and markets continued to thrive. Such industries were ceramics, glass, leather for shoes and gloves, and soap. But they did not create an inflow of foreign money, and it was such money that was needed to pay for the imports coming into Spain.

* The decline in both agriculture and industry affected trade. Imports increased. These included not only luxury goods but also basic necessities such as grain, textiles, hardware, paper, and the better quality naval stores. But as fewer ships were being built in Spain, this increased trade was in the hands of foreigners. The position became worse in the second half of the seventeenth century when a series of commercial treaties was made with Holland, France and England. These enabled foreign goods to enter Spain more cheaply, and further damaged what manufacturing industry remained.

The value of Spain's imports was much greater than that of her exports. This was not a major problem while she was receiving large amounts of silver from America, but it did matter once the flow of silver diminished. Although there had been a great rise in the amount of silver coming into Spain from the American colonies between 1562 and 1592, this levelled off between 1593 and 1622, before going into sharp decline. A major reason for this was that, by the seventeenth century, the Spanish American colonies no longer required the type of goods that Spain could supply as they were producing them for themselves. What they did require were goods, especially fine cloth and high quality metal ware, that Spain could not supply. In theory, the colonists should have imported these products by way of Spain, but it was much cheaper to smuggle them in directly from England, France and Holland, and the authorities were powerless to stop them. An additional factor was that large sums of money had to be kept in the colonies to provide for defence against increasing attacks, especially by the Dutch, the French and the English.

* Finance had been a serious problem from at least the middle of the sixteenth century. Philip II had left enormous debts to his son. Castile had been the only part of the Empire over which he had had enough control to force it to grant the substantial amounts of money that he required. The situation was worsened by Philip III's personal extravagance and gifts. Greater attempts were made under Philip IV to reduce expenditure. The number of gifts the king made to such people as widows and former army officers was reduced, and the costs of the royal

household decreased. Salaries of courtiers and officials were also reduced. Attempts were made to prevent foreign manufactured goods coming into the country. But the expense of re-starting wars in so many areas in the 1620s was far greater than any savings which could be made.

Various attempts were made to stave off bankruptcy. In 1599 a *vellon* coinage, made of pure copper rather than silver, was issued. More was issued in 1602, 1603, 1617 and 1621. By 1650 copper made up over 98% of coinage in common use. But the government itself suffered as a consequence of such debasement. The true worth of the income it received within Spain was now much less than it had previously been. Debts outside Spain had to be paid in silver and this became more difficult as the amount of silver bullion coming from America was falling. Between 1596 and 1600 13.7 million ducats were received by the crown. This fell to 5.5 million in 1626–30 and 2 million in 1646–50.

Payment of debts was therefore suspended again in 1607, 1627, 1647, 1652 and 1662. This was no solution to the problem as each time it happened the size of debt increased. By 1667 three-quarters of current income was used to pay debts.

New sources of income were looked for, mainly in Castile. In 1624 the first of several 'free gifts' were levied. Crown lands were sold. The *lances* tax (1631) allowed nobles to pay a sum of money instead of having to go on military service. All those in official posts had to contribute half a year's income to the Crown in 1630. From 1636 a stamp tax and a tax on playing cards were introduced. Attempts to introduce a salt tax failed, however, when they led to riots. These measures, of course, did not address the major problem of the monarchy living well beyond its means. They did no more than make a desperate situation slightly better.

By 1664 the crown owed 21.6 million ducats. Philip IV had nothing to leave his son but an enormous debt and an empty treasury, and there was little prospect of the situation being improved.

5 Was there a Decline of Spain in the Seventeenth Century?

The traditional view of Spanish history in this period was that Spain rose to greatness during the sixteenth century and suffered a continuous and complete decline in the seventeenth century. This interpretation stressed the contrast between the Spain of Charles I and Philip II as the most powerful country in Europe, and that of Philip III and IV, as the power that was rapidly overtaken by Holland, France and England.

Spain was considered to have declined economically, militarily, politically and socially. Her kings were believed to be weak, lacking in ability, and dominated by their favourites. They were regarded as extravagant. There was said to be little investment in industry, trade and agriculture. The debasement of the *vellon* coinage, the increase of the *alcabala* and the tax on food were said to have ruined the country. It was also said that economic problems had been exacerbated by the expulsion of the *moriscos*; that Spain was too inward looking because of her strong support for Catholicism; that the Inquisition made it difficult for new ideas to be accepted; that involvement in wars hastened the decline by the enormous cost involved; and that Spain's military reputation was destroyed by failures in the Battle of the Downs and the Battle of Rocroi.

Is this an accurate picture? Was the contrast so stark? Was Spain's position so strong in the sixteenth century? Historians usually refer nowadays to the seeds of the seventeenth century problems being sown in the sixteenth century. Spain was already suffering economically. There were repeated bankruptcies. By the end of the century the population had already started to fall. Spain, particularly from 1580 onwards, was over-committed in military ventures, most notably in France. Some historians see the turning point as coming when Charles I involved Spain more heavily in European affairs on becoming Holy Roman Emperor. Certainly financial crises were apparent from the time of his reign. If Spain was in difficulties in at least some respects in the sixteenth century, should one talk of a decline coming in the seventeenth century?

Yet it is quite clear that Spain was in crisis for much of the seventeenth century. This was apparent especially in financial and economic affairs. The kings and their ministers had enormous problems in raising enough money to finance their wars. And there can be little doubt that the effects of the drop in population were extremely damaging. It became more difficult for Spain to win victories at sea or on land. Within the peninsula, Portugal and Catalonia revolted successfully against Spanish rule, and the Spanish Empire was beginning to break up. In 1648 the independence of the Netherlands was recognised. In 1659 Roussillon, Cerdagne and Artois were lost to France.

Some historians believe that a more balanced view is possible if they set the history of Spain during the sixteenth and early seventeenth centuries more in the context of European history as a whole. Was Spain's strong military and political position in Europe in the sixteenth century due to France's involvement in religious wars from 1559 onwards? In the early seventeenth century Europe as a whole experienced a 'general crisis'. Some historians see Spain's economic depression during these years as being similar to the economic conditions prevailing in other European countries – except that her depression lasted longer and was more severe – and they stress that in political and military affairs, Spain still retained a relatively important position in Europe.

Several historians have guided us into asking not why Spain declined but why she was able to survive for so long. The administration continued to work and to be effective in obtaining just enough money, men and supplies to fight wars well into the seventeenth century. The majority of the Empire remained Spanish. Catalonia became part of Spain again. Literature and art continued to flourish. This was the period of Cervantes's 'Don Quixote' and of the playwrights Lope de Vega and

Calderon. Some of the finest paintings of the period were produced by artists such as Velasquez, Zurbaran and Murillo. Spain may have slipped from being regarded as the pre-eminent power in Europe, but care should be taken not to exaggerate the change. It was not until the nineteenth century that she could be accurately described as one of the minor European countries.

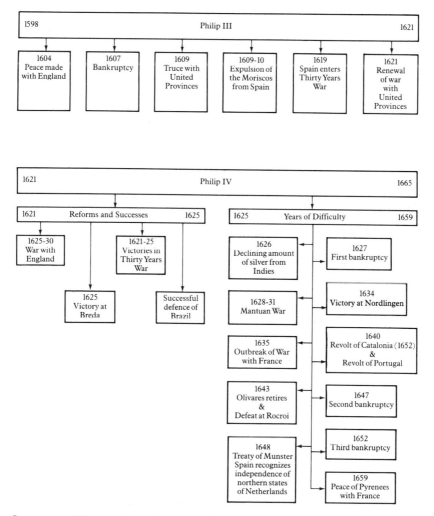

Summary – The Decline of Spain, 1598–1665

Making notes on 'The Decline of Spain? 1598–1643'

When making notes on this chapter try to decide how far each of the topics covered could be considered to show Spain in decline.

1. Contemporary criticisms of Spain's position in the early seventeenth century. List these under the following headings:
1.1. Society
1.2. Economic
1.3. Military
2. Philip III
2.1. Personal qualities
2.2. The *valido* – general comments for and against the use of a *valido* and a brief consideration of the abilities of Lerma
2.3. The conciliar system – how far were improvements made under Philip III?
2.4. The juntas
2.5. The abilities of Philip's ministers
2.6. The expulsion of the *moriscos*
3. Philip IV
3.1. Personal qualities
3.2. Olivares – character, aims, reforms, retirement
4. The Empire and foreign policy
   Draw up a time chart for this, making a brief note on the importance of each event mentioned, and whether it was a failure or success for Spain
4.1. Philip III's relations with foreign countries
4.2. The Netherlands under Philip III
4.3. Involvement in Thirty Years War
4.4. Olivares's aims – Union of Arms
4.5. The Netherlands from 1621
4.6. Importance of the year 1626
4.7. Mantua and its importance
4.8. Outbreak of war with France – reasons and importance
4.9. Significance of the Battle of the Downs and Rocroi
4.10. Catalonia – why it revolted and importance of this
4.11. Portugal – why it revolted, importance and reasons for success
4.12. Castile
4.13. Foreign policy 1643–1659
5. The economy
5.1. Population
5.2. Agriculture
5.3. Industry
5.4. Trade
5.5. Finance

Answering essay questions on 'The Decline of Spain? 1598–1643'

The majority of the essay questions on this topic focus on the reasons for the decline of Spain either during the reign of Philip III, or during the reign of Philip IV, or both:

> 'Account for the decline of Spain in the reign of Philip III and Philip IV.'
>
> 'How far was economic failure responsible for the decline of Spain?'

Make a list of the topics that you think are important in explaining the decline of Spain. Then make brief notes for each, including the examples you will use as illustrations. Which do you think were the most fundamental causes? Indicate this by numbering the topics in order of importance. When writing up the essay from your outline, remember that you must comment on why you think each particular point is a reason for the decline.

The second essay suggests one particular cause for the decline. Deal with this first and try to assess its importance. As the essay includes the words 'How far . . .', you need to include all the other factors from your list, trying to assess the responsibility of *each* for the decline.

Questions also tend to be set on Olivares:

> 'Why and how far did Olivares fail?'
>
> 'He had grand ideas which he was unable to carry out.' Consider this view of the achievements of Olivares.'

Such questions involve looking more closely at a person and his responsibility for failure or success. In such questions you usually need to look at:

a. personality and character – in what ways did they affect his work?
b. aims – what was Olivares trying to accomplish?
c. methods – what policies did he follow to try to put his aims into effect?
d. success – how much was achieved?
e. causes – why was his degree of success achieved?

In answering the first question you would tackle 'how far' before explaining 'why'. Which aspects listed above would help you to answer 'how far'? Which would help answer 'why'? Both parts of the essay would require comment on Olivares's aims. Had he set himself an impossible task? If you can, identify several criteria for measuring his success.

The second question is of the 'contentious statement' type. The most effective way of answering such a question is to construct a two-part essay. Begin by presenting all the arguments you can think of to support the statement. Then deal with the other possible factors. Conclude by indicating where you think the truth lies.

Source-based questions on 'The Decline of Spain? 1598–1643'

1 Seventeenth century extracts on 'decline'

Read the extracts on pages 86–7 and answer the following questions:

a) What do these documents say about the condition of Spain in the early years of the seventeenth century?

b) What explanation does the second extract give as to why Spain was 'as ruined and as poor as it is now'?

c) How persuasive in its tone and vocabulary do you consider the third extract to be?

d) Making use of your own knowledge, how far do you consider the reasons given in the second extract to be an accurate explanation for the problems Spain was experiencing?

2 The ministers of Philip III (page 89)

a) How do these documents differ in their assessments of Philip III's ministers?

b) How do the two documents differ in their tone and vocabulary? Which of the two do you consider would have had the greater influence at the time?

c) Giving reasons for your answers, explain which of these extracts a historian is more likely to consider reliable.

3 Olivares's plans for unity in the Empire

Read the extract on page 92 and answer the following questions:

a) What does Olivares mean by saying that Philip IV should 'become king of Spain'?

b) In what ways would Olivares make this suggestion acceptable to non-Castilians?

c) If a non-Castilian read only the first part of Olivares's paper ('The most important thing . . . in the world'), what do you consider his reaction would be? In what ways does this indicate to you the difficulties to a historian of only using extracts from documents, or a small number of documents?

3 'The Knight's Dream'

Look at the picture on page 100 and answer the following questions:

a) What objects does the knight dream about?

b) What symbolic meaning can be attached to each of these objects?

c) What reasons is the artist indicating for the 'decline' of Spain?

d) Using your own knowledge, how far do you consider the artist is accurate in his assessment of the causes of Spain's difficulties in the early years of the seventeenth century?

e) Explain the problems that a historian encounters in using paintings such as this one as evidence?

Further Reading

There are three general histories of Spain which, although not intended for A-Level students, could be read, in part at least, to gain further understanding of the period.

One book which is still highly popular, although first published in 1963, is:

J. H. Elliott, *Imperial Spain 1469–1716* (Edward Arnold 1963).

This concentrates on Spain itself. It does not set Spanish history firmly into its European context but deals in detail with such topics as religion, the economy and the Spanish court.

Well worth using selectively for its more up to date interpretations is:

H. Kamen, *Spain 1469–1714* (Longman 1983).

As well as giving a clear outline on political history, it also includes details of religious matters, and social and economic history.

A very readable general history is:

A. Dominguez Ortiz, *The Golden Age of Spain* (Weidenfeld and Nicolson 1971).

This provides interesting background reading on literature and the arts, religious issues, economic and social conditions, as well as political narrative.

Many biographies have been published on Philip II. One which is easy to read and gives an illuminating personal view of Philip II is:

G. Parker, *Philip II* (Hutchinson 1979).

A most recent biography of Olivares, which will probably prove to be the standard work on the subject is:

J. H. Elliott, *Olivares* (Yale 1986).

A highly readable article on Philip IV appeared in *History Today* in March, 1981. A-Level students would also find it worthwhile to read the useful summary of recent work on the decline of Spain which is to be found in *G. Parker's* article in *History Today*, April, 1984.

Sources on *Spain: Rise and Decline, 1474–1643*

Relatively little source material has been published in English on sixteenth and seventeenth century Spain. The following book has some material relevant to Spain during the reign of Philip II:

1   **J. C. Davis** (ed), *Pursuit of Power: Venetian Ambassadors – reports on Spain Turkey and France in the age of Philip II 1560–1600* (New York, 1970).
2   **K. Leach**, *Documents and Debates, Sixteenth Century Europe* (Macmillan, 1980) – includes some documents on Spain during this period.
    Apart from these, a number of short extracts are to be found in:
3   **H. Kamen**, *Spain 1469–1714* (Longman, 1983).
4   **E. Grierson**, *King of Two Worlds: Philip II of Spain* (Collins, 1974).
5   **P. Pierson**, *Philip II of Spain* (Thames and Hudson, 1975).

Acknowledgements

The author and publishers would like to thank the following for their permission to use copyright illustrations:
Cover: M.A.S., Barcelona and p.56; Mansell Collection Ltd.: p.74; Collins Publishers: p.100.

Index